A Little Less Conversation

Practical Books for Smart Marketers from PMP

Market Research

The 4Cs of Truth in Communication: *How to Identify, Discuss, Evaluate and Present Stand-out, Effective Communication*

The Art of Strategic Listening: *Finding Market Intelligence through Blogs and other Social Media*

Consumer Insights 2.0: *How Smart Companies Apply Customer Knowledge to the Bottom Line*

Dominators, Cynics, and Wallflowers: *Practical Strategies for Moderating Meaningful Focus Groups*

The Mirrored Window: *Focus Groups from a Moderator's Point of View*

Moderating to the Max! *A Full-Tilt Guide to Creative, Insightful Focus Groups and Depth Interviews*

Religion in a Free Market: *Religious and Non-Religious Americans—Who, What, Why, Where*

Why People Buy Things They Don't Need

Mature Market/ Baby Boomers

Advertising to Baby Boomers

After Fifty: *How the Baby Boom Will Redefine the Mature Market*

After Sixty: *Marketing to Baby Boomers Reaching Their Big Transition Years*

Baby Boomers and Their Parents: *Surprising Findings about Their Lifestyles, Mindsets, and Well-Being*

The Boomer Heartbeat: *Capturing the Heartbeat of the Baby Boomers Now and in the Future*

Marketing to Leading-Edge Baby Boomers

Multicultural

Beyond Bodegas: *Developing a Retail Relationship with Hispanic Customers*

Hispanic Marketing Grows Up: *Exploring Perceptions and Facing Realities*

Hispanic Customers for Life: *A Fresh Look at Acculturation*

India Business: *Finding Opportunities in this Big Emerging Market*

Latinization: *How Latino Culture Is Transforming the U.S.*

Marketing to American Latinos: *A Guide to the In-Culture Approach, Parts I & II*

The Whole Enchilada: *Hispanic Marketing 101*

What's Black About It? *Insights to Increase Your Share of a Changing African-American Market*

Youth Markets

The Great Tween Buying Machine: *Marketing to Today's Tweens*

The Kids Market: *Myths & Realities*

Marketing to the New Super Consumer: Mom & Kid

Marketing Strategy/Management

A Clear Eye for Branding: *Straight Talk on Today's Most Powerful Business Concept*

A Knight's Code of Business: *How to Achieve Character and Competence in the Corporate World*

Beyond the Mission Statement: *Why Cause-Based Communications Lead to True Success*

Brand Busters: *7 Common Mistakes Marketers Make*

Marketing Insights to Help Your Business Grow

Outsmart the MBA Clones *The Alternative Guide to Competitive Strategy, Marketing, and Branding*

Using Choice Modeling to Supercharge Your Business: *The Essential Non-Technical Guide*

A Little Less Conversation

Connecting with Customers

in a Noisy World

Tom Asacker

PMP

Paramount Market Publishing, Inc.

Published by Paramount Market Publishing, Inc.
950 Danby Road, Suite 136, Ithaca, New York 14850
www.paramountbooks.com
Printed in the United States of America

ISBN 13: 978-0-9801745-2-6
ISBN10: 0-9801745-2-x

10 9 8 7 6 5 4 3 2 1

This one's for the doers.

Contents

The future is disorder. A door like this has opened up only five or six times since we got up on our hind legs. It's the best possible time to be alive, when almost everything you thought you knew is wrong.

Valentine, in Tom Stoppard's play *Arcadia*

Introduction

"So what's the answer?" I could sense that question playing on the mind of the weary-eyed executive sitting directly in front of me. I've picked up that same vibe during countless presentations over the past few years: *"Tell us what to do to attract and retain customers. What's the formula? Give us the solution."*

But this time was different, much different. On this particular Thursday morning in April, I was presenting to, arguably, the most storied marketing company in the history of the world. Yes, the prophetic day had arrived. The complexity and rapid change of today's contemporary marketplace had finally overwhelmed even the brightest minds in the biggest and best companies in America.

Yogi Berra once quipped, "The future ain't what it used to be." If you look beneath the surface of Yogi's seemingly absurd aphorism, you'll discover an insightful truth about succeeding in the 21ST century marketplace. And it's this: you can no longer benchmark and model the past in order to be successful in the future, because the future is changing too quickly and unpredictably (It ain't what it used to be). Trying to do so will lead to your inevitable downfall, as smartly described by Professor Donald Sull in the *Harvard Business Review*: "Many leading companies plummet from the pinnacle of success to the depths of failure when market conditions change. Because they're para-lyzed? To the contrary, because they engage in too much activity of the wrong kind. Success breeds active inertia, and active inertia breeds failure."

A head-down, plow-ahead mentality is deadly in a rapidly changing marketplace. You may believe that you know what's happening around you, but like driving the same road to work every day, you've simply become hypnotized by your extremely narrow, short-term interest and unchanging point of view. Instead, realize that, like it or not, today's shifting marketplace is like one of those car racing video games: there is no actual car. It's the *road* to success that is moving right in front of your eyes. The only way to make sense of it and, hopefully, be successful is to pay attention and move with it.

"Okay," you may be thinking, *"but why another book on customers? People are still just people after all."* No, they are not. The people of mature, 21ST century marketplaces are much different than those of years past. They are also unlike consumers in emerging markets: they are more experienced, skeptical, savvy, and connected. They have much different attention spans, mindsets, motivations, media habits, sources of social influence and, most impor-tantly, marketplace desires. But most customer-focused business books still espouse 1950's absolutist rhetoric and western, mass market concepts like, "positioning," "Unique Selling Proposition" and "top-of-mind awareness."

There are no absolutes when dealing with customers. It's not an objective process, like a physical science where you try to influence the behavior of chemicals in a beaker.

Especially today, it's a subjective and complicated blend of art and science where you're trying to influence people's feelings. So the goal of this little book, like my previous one, *A Clear Eye for Branding,* is to cut through all of that noise and help you feel what's really happening in the marketplace for products, services, entertainment, causes, and ideas. I want to shake up your present worldview and help you see a new meaning about how to attract customers, and engage, seduce, and delight them; a meaning which, by the way, transcends communication.

I'll be using the word "customer" throughout this book to refer to any person involved in examining, evaluating, purchasing, using, or recommending anything of value. You may refer to said person as consumer, prospect, user, member, client, constituent, donor, patient, resident, audience, voter, fan, citizen, or some other idiom. And that's fine, so long as you embrace the sentiment in the late, great ad man, David Ogilvy's adage, "The consumer is not a moron, she is your wife," and appreciate the fact that she is also your child's teacher, your colleague, neighbor, future employer, prolific blogger, political leader, and media maven.

So let's get to it. Let me set the stage for the hypothetical, yet reality-inspired dialog that's to follow. I've just finished presenting my concepts at a major conference, and I've arrived at the airport the next morning to discover, once again, that my flight has been cancelled. I'm standing at the ticket counter, my head hanging in disgust, when I notice an empathetic, elderly man of the cloth standing to my left. Happy reading!

A Little Less
Conversation

One: Awake at the Wheel

*Everyone gets so much information all day long
that they lose their common sense.*

Gertrude Stein

Tom: I cannot believe this!

Elderly man: *What's wrong my son?*

My flight has been cancelled . . . again. I have to rebook on a later one.

I'm sure everything will be fine.

I hope so.

So, do you know why, when the Messiah returns, he is coming back on a donkey?

Huh? No . . . why?

Because the airlines are unreliable.

[Tom smiles] That's a good one. Thanks!

You're welcome. Well, I have to go now. You have a safe trip.

You too!

[Executive behind Tom] *That was pretty funny.*

Yeah . . . he's certainly a wise, old man. He totally knocked me out of my negative frame of mind.

Hey, weren't you our keynote speaker last night?

Yes, I was. How are you?

Doing okay. Although my flight was just delayed, too.

You too? I'm sorry to hear that.

I've gotten used to it. Listen, do you want to go grab a bite to eat?

Sounds great. But it's on me.

I'll tell you what. How 'bout I buy, in exchange for you letting me pick your brain a bit?

It's a deal!

How does that pub over there look to you?

Great! Let's go.

The helter-skelter marketplace

So Tom, I was struck by the sense of urgency you expressed in your talk. You said that it's critical to gain a visceral understanding of today's radically new customer mindset. What precisely is so new?

A lot. Customers are not only inundated with a kudzu-like explosion of product and service offerings and outlets; they are also drowning in information, media choices, and commercial messages. It's like a perfect storm of influences and confusion.

So, it's today's increased level of competition that has made it so much more difficult to capture people's attention and succeed?

Sort of, but I don't like to look at it from that perspective. Think about the word "competition;" it's from the Latin *competere,* meaning "seeking or striving together." The competitive paradigm forces you to both compare yourself to, and align your thinking with, others. And inevitably, you begin focusing on the wrong things.

It's like running a road race. At the start of a race, you have a panoptic view; you're aware of everything and everyone. But as the race progresses, you tend to focus narrowly on those few runners nearest to you—your "competitors." Instead of viewing it from this classic competitive angle, try seeing it from a customer's viewpoint.

Which is?

Like I said: too much choice, too much conflicting information, and not enough time to deal with it all. In the United States alone, there are dozens of brands of toothpaste, hundreds of car models, thousands of organized religious groups and tens of thousands of non-profits. Google any product or service you can think of and take a look at the shear number of results.

So, there's more choice. I'm pretty sure that everyone is aware of that fact.

Perhaps. So, let me ask you. When you shop for groceries, about how many different brands do you think you purchase?

On a typical shopping trip? I don't know, maybe 20 or 30?

Okay, that's close to the average. And how many brands—different items—do you think there are to choose from in a typical grocery store?

I have no idea. A lot.

More than a lot. Somewhere between thirty and fifty *thousand*, and there's a plethora of new ones, and ones designed to look new, appearing every day. That's just at a supermarket. Toss in clothing, electronics, books, restaurants, hotels, sporting goods, financial products, drugs, jewelry, insurance, professional services, vacation destinations, and so forth along with club stores, dollar stores, convenience stores, specialty stores, TV shopping, direct marketing, the Internet, etc., and you'll quickly get a *feel* for the condition.

I guess I've never really thought of it all that much.

Of course you haven't. Like most people, you're not consciously *aware* of it. You simply deal with it. And this overwhelming amount of choice is just one aspect of the mental storm that has totally upended customers' way of thinking about, and choosing, products, services, entertainment and causes. There are others.

Like?

Everything has changed

Let me give you five major trends that have intensified of late and have brought about this major change in how customers think, and thus how and what they choose. As we've discussed, the first one is that today's customer is supersaturated with choice. Think about the sprawl of options that customers face to make a simple bowl of Cheerios cereal; from regular Cheerios, Honey Nut, Berry Burst, Yogurt Burst, MultiGrain, Fruity, Frosted, and Apple Cinnamon to choices of whole milk, fat-free skimmed milk, protein-enriched fat-free, 1 percent, 2 percent, lactose-free, vitamin D-fortified, organic, soy milk, *yadayadayada*. And the flood of marketplace offerings and channels is not about to subside any time soon, because the rapid development and introduction of new products is essential to satisfy customers' bottomless appetite for novelty.

In which particular industries? Consumer products? Technology?

All industries. People are attracted to, and love to talk about, what's new and valuable; be it a new restaurant, new movie, new cell phone, new shade of lipstick, or new social networking platform. Marketers are well aware that attraction and word-of-mouth are vital in an economy of abundance, so they'll continue to release scads of new and, hopefully, improved offerings at a breakneck pace.

Companies have released scores of new products and services over the past few years, and many of them are struggling.

Exactly. Newness may cause people to pause, because they typically filter for new information to decide if it's relevant. But—and this is a critical but—they won't spend a second more of their time, or a penny more of their money, unless they can quickly intuit its compelling value.

What's in it for them. Okay, I'm with you.

It's a bit more complex and nuanced than you're probably thinking, but let's keep going. We'll come back to this notion of "value" in a few minutes. The second trend affecting today's customer mindset, and we've touched upon it briefly, is the overwhelming amount of information and, increasingly, the number of media platforms available to customers. For example, the Internet is now populated with tens of *billions* of web pages. While we've been sitting here, hundreds of thousands of new pages have been added. You've heard of a blog, right?

Sure. It's an online diary of sorts.

That's right, although today's blogs are increasingly used as tools for outreach to a specific audience. Anyway, there are more than 70 million blogs presently being tracked and close to 150,000 new blogs launch daily.

Incredible.

That same information glut exists in old media as well. There were close to 300,000 books published last year; over 7,000 of them were business books. One daily issue of the *New York Times* contains more information than someone who lived in the 17TH century was exposed to during his or her entire lifetime. There are tens of thousands of magazine titles. We now have satellite and HD radio in addition to AM, FM, streaming and podcasts, and my friend's *TV Guide* resembles an old Sears Roebuck catalogue.

[Exec smiles] *Fifty-seven channels and nothin' on.*

A Springsteen fan! Me too! But "The Boss" hasn't seen anything yet. In the very near future, there'll be an almost infinite number of channels with nothin' on. Television, radio, and the Internet are all going to converge providing access to streaming audio and online video right from your TV remote, which invariably will have a little search box built right in. However, there's something paradoxical about this "wealth" of information.

What's that?

It's all conflicting. You find me a piece of information, and I'll find you information that refutes yours, or at the very least, calls the validity of yours into question.

About anything? C'mon.

Just about. You've probably heard that Pluto is no longer a planet, right? It's been deplanetized, except in New Mexico where the state legislature has reinstated it. And there's still a group of people who are convinced that the world is actually flat. They've even posted scientific data on their website to back up their claims. But let me be a bit more serious. Do you believe that television viewing is good or bad for kids?

I'd guess bad, but I have a distinct feeling that you can give me data to support both propositions.

Indeed. In fact, I can pretty much find "information" that will support or contest any proposition from the legitimacy of human's influence on global warming to the health benefits of eating fruits and vegetables. And that's my point: This flood of conflicting information is contributing to a particular customer mindset.

Which is?

Hold on for just a few more minutes. Let me give you the other three trends, which should help to make it very clear. The third major trend, which the Internet has enabled and is fueling, is radical transparency and message amplification. The second generation of web-based services referred to as Web 2.0, which emphasizes social networking, online communities, collaboration, interactivity, and user-created content, has created a hyper-connected marketplace. Customers are increasingly sharing information and opinions about products, services, people, and organizations. They're posting photos, videos, reviews, recommendations, prices, and thoughts on anything and everything from new product designs and stocks, to corporate behavior and inner company workings. The whole concept of word-of-mouth has been turbocharged, turning the Internet into both a bullhorn for customer complaints and a massive market research channel.

I totally agree, and we're working hard to participate in that growing online conversation. Our company's social networking platform gets hundreds of hits a month, and generates a lot of valuable comments from existing and prospective customers.

That's great! Customers yearn to participate and to be heard. Engaging in dialogue demonstrates that you care about them and their opinions. Just don't delude yourself into believing that they care as much about you and your views, as they want you to care about theirs. Which brings me to the fourth trend, and the best way for me to explain it is to share a little story with you. A few years back, I was in Germany presenting to a large, European-based company that was interested in expanding its market presence in the U.S. At one point during my talk, I displayed an image of a can of Chicken of the Sea tuna on the screen and before I could utter a word, the room was surreptitiously buzzing with conversation and laughter.

About the tuna?

That's what I was wondering, so I asked a gentleman in the front row. He smiled, shrugged his shoulders and pointed to the screen, *"What is it?"* he asked in his European accent. I turned and glanced at the screen, then looked back at the roomful of puzzled people and replied, *"A can of tuna fish."* *"We know that,"* he replied matter-of-factly. *"But what is* chicken *from the sea tuna. What does that mean? There is no chicken in the sea."*

[Exec smiling] *Sounds like a Jerry Seinfeld skit.*

It was pretty funny. They had never seen that brand of canned tuna fish, and the name totally baffled them. So I launched into an historical account of U.S. mass marketing during the post-World War II economic boom, and described the difference between yesterday's uninformed, submissive consumers—people whose choice of tuna was actually influenced by the brand name Chicken of the Sea—and today's highly active and skeptical discerners of marketing.

The fourth trend?

Customers want control

It's this: Customers "get it." They're now in the driver's seat. Not only are they well informed and savvy, but many even want to participate in the very marketing they used to passively consume. You see, there used to be a media divider between companies and customers that marketers used to control the trip, like the divider between the limo driver and her passengers. When I was a kid, my Dad read the morning paper while having his coffee, listened to his favorite radio station on his drive to work, and, in the evening, we all sat together and watched our favorite television shows. And, by the way, we didn't have a remote control, so even if we didn't particularly like what we were watching at the time, we watched anyway. We were too lazy to get up and change the channel.

Marketers hid behind this curtain, broadcasting their messages to, what was truly a mass of naïve, passive consumers. Marketers took customers where *they* wanted to take them and customers just sat in the backseat like well-behaved children. Take a look at some ads from the 1940s and 1950s. I saw a reproduction of a full-page print add with a photograph of a physician and the words, *"More Doctors Smoke Camels than any other cigarette!"*

C'mon.

I'm serious. Consumers were conditioned to believe them. Once upon a time, when products and services of obvious differentiated quality and value were popping up like weeds in a field, consumers were predisposed to believe all kinds of advertising claims, both overt and subtle ones. And since belief leads to action, sales of those advertised goods increased as well. Heinz's relish was, in the mind of the consumer, a perceivable improvement over generic relish. And in fact, sensory evidence—a full jar, no grit to chew, consistent texture and taste—proved it out. The product lived up to both its marketing claim and to the company's founding principle: "To do a common thing uncommonly well, brings success." It was actually a better product.

The same was true for many other modern wonders of the American age of mass production including the radio, telephone, automobile, television, washing machine, dishwasher, and air conditioner. They were special products that, in fact, changed the world and improved people's lives. During those heady marketing times, consumers were predisposed—based on their memories of past experiences—to endorse and thereby become behaviorally susceptible to advertising's representational content. Times were indeed very good for advertisers, as well they should have been. Then something happened.

Before I tell you what, let's go back about 300 years. Around that time, the great Dutch philosopher Benedictus de Spinoza postulated that to comprehend something was also to believe it. For example, if you said, *"My eyes are brown,"* I would simultaneously understand *and* believe your statement. To disbelieve your statement would require a subsequent act of rejection, based on logic or, in this case, sensory evidence. Recent research in social and cognitive psychology suggests that Spinoza was right: The acceptance of an idea is part of the automatic comprehension of that idea, and the rejection of an idea occurs subsequent to, and with more effort than, its acceptance.

What does that have to do with customers' mindsets?

Everything. During the heyday of mass marketing, consumers were easy to reach and they were predisposed to comprehend, accept, and act upon advertising for two primary reasons. First, to construct their views of reality, people combine what they sense with what they already think, feel, and believe. During that time, customers' memories of past representations of advertising supported its acceptance; the stuff really was an improvement. Second, they *wanted* to believe. It felt good to believe that by simply buying stuff they could become more successful, desirable, live longer, and be happier.

People wanted *to believe what advertisers told them?*

Of course they did. People are happiest when they're imagining happiness and, in their minds at that time, there was very little downside to believing. Think of it this way: If you say to me, *"Tom. You're the smartest guy I know,"* I will probably choose to believe you. Why? Because it feels good to believe you, and there is no risk involved in believing. Also, it would likely be difficult and time consuming to disprove your statement since I would have to understand what you mean by "smart," work with you to list everyone you know, and agree upon the best test for smarts, among other things. All in all, it benefits me to simply believe without verification, unless, of course, past representations by you have proven to be complete hogwash or a waste of my time.

Like a lot of more recent advertising.

Right. Our brains are pattern-mad, expectation-creation machines. We look into our memory for similar experiences that are contextually relevant in order to predict the meaning, and thus the future, of new ones. In essence, we speed read our environment and fill in the blanks, typically without being aware of what we're doing. For example, when you returned to your hotel room last night and found a triangle folded into the toilet paper, what did it mean to you?

It meant that someone had cleaned the bathroom.

What it really meant was that someone folded a triangle into the toilet paper.

[Exec smiles] *True.*

What other predictions did you make based upon that visual stimulus, that clue? What else did you expect?

Let's see. If it was the first thing I noticed upon entering my room, I would have predicted that the bed was made and that the tub was cleaned. And that I wouldn't be disturbed by room service. Things like that.

Your eyes (your senses) joined with what you believe (your feelings), in this case based on your memory of similar past experiences, to create your perception of reality (your thoughts) and to predict your probable future (your expectations). You see, your memory is like a train of associations. Once a particular train has been set in motion by some contextual signal, like the triangle, it runs on a set track, quietly below your level of consciousness. And that's how customers choose. They continually map the marketplace, using their memories of direct experiences and on chunks of information—like advertising—in an attempt to predict their probable futures.

So yes, customers accepted advertising when it primed their memories and signaled valid and positive associations, or even when they had no way to verify them and simply wanted them to be true. To a limited extent, they still behave this way. But what do you think happens when customers become overloaded with stuff, inundated with options, and bedazzled by information. How do they even decide what to pay attention to when time is such a costly currency?

I suppose they pay attention to what's relevant to them.

Experience elicits meaning

That's everyone's goal, yes. But how do they go about it? How do they screen for relevance?

I'm not sure. How?

They sense something and then quickly and imperceptibly access their stored memory, which sets the train of associations in motion. Then they watch where the train takes them; i.e., ignore it, get more information, try it, etc. Their feelings and thoughts link together, instructing them what action to take. In essence, they screen and reason with their guts.

Like the fight or flight response?

Sometimes. More often though, it's a more complex, albeit rapid, processing of information. One that becomes fine-tuned through experience. I once read about an experiment with master chess players that showed that they could glance at the position of pieces on a chessboard during a game and later perfectly recall the precise position of every piece. However, if they were shown a chessboard with randomly arranged pieces, their memories failed. It wasn't a photographic memory that gave each of them an edge. It was their past experiences. They could chunk information into meaningful patterns and recall those patterns for later use.

The same is true of customers' marketplace gaming. They've become active discerners and meaning-makers of marketplace information. They easily recall memories of paying attention to information that turned out to be irrelevant, or of responding to ads that claimed "specialness." They quickly conjure up images of products and services that they were led to believe would improve their lives and make them happier. And what patterns do you think emerge?

Smoke and mirrors.

Right. In more cases than not, they find sameness and disappointment. And since people's brains abhor dissonance, they easily solve this information problem by tuning out the source of the conflicting information. So now, customers know the words to most marketing songs; they simply don't feel the music.

And people don't dance to lyrics.

Exactly! Add to that the fact that the media landscape has splintered into a plethora of platforms and sophisticated consumers are spending less time with traditional media, and the few marketing messages consumers *do* receive are suspect, at best.

So customers are predisposed not *to believe commercial messages?*

Many of them, yes. Their past experiences have shaped

what they see and expect. Like skilled chess players, customers have been conditioned to know exactly what an advertiser's "position" means to them. And with the game clock moving in a rapidly changing environment like today's marketplace, customers are compelled to play quickly. They scan and detect new "positions," use past experience to determine their meaning, decide what to do, and then learn from their choices. They don't have time for intellectual rigor, nor the option of being frequently wrong.

I'm a little confused. Do customers consciously evaluate marketing messages or not?

It's not an either-or question. Marketing messages are processed, and accepted or rejected, primarily by our subconscious minds. However, customers are raising more and more company communication to a conscious level as well. So when they *do* pause to experience an ad, direct mail piece, press release, website, or other marketing material they pay attention to every nuance. Consider the fact that deconstructing and evaluating Super Bowl commercials is now many people's favorite part of the game.

I've even seen commercials created by consumers.

That's my point. People don't passively sit around and consume commercial messages like they used to. Either they tune them out, by channel surfing, multitasking, or removing them from their media content, or, if the product or service is highly relevant to them, they get involved in some way. They may do detailed "research" on the Internet, or participate on a blog or some other online forum like your customers do. Or, they may email their friends for their opinions or even create and post their own advertisements or other content. Sometimes they demonstrate their affinity for the company or showcase their creative talent, and at other times they mock the company's ad or highlight a poor experience they've recently had with the organization.

Customers know all about the little man behind the curtain. So marketers must respect their intelligence and engage them either by pulling back the curtain and inviting them in to play with the levers, or by creating something useful or meaningful that customers find value in and can share with their friends. Either way, marketers should never forget that customers fully understand the game that is being played, and that they are choosing to play it the way that best fits *their* fancy.

Okay, so customers are inundated with choice, drowning in an insurmountable amount of typically conflicting information, hyper-connected, and sharing information about people, brands, and companies on the Internet, and actively discerning, and participating in, marketing. What could possibly be left?

Something fairly obvious, if you're thinking like a customer instead of a marketer, and it's this: Customers increasingly don't trust businesses or the people who run them. At least that's the state of consumer trust in the U.S., as measured by various researchers.

Because of their experience with advertising?

Sure, that's part of it, but it runs much deeper. Think back to the turn of the century and consider what people have been exposed to over the subsequent years from the Enron debacle and the scandals at companies like World-Com, Adelphia, Arthur Andersen, and Global Crossing, to the Catholic Church disgrace, the Major League Baseball steroid scandal, various transgressions by political leaders and celebrities, plagiarism by newspaper reporters, and the mortgage lending scandal. Even Martha Stuart was sent to prison for lying.

Wow, if we can't trust Martha Stuart, whom can we trust?

[Tom smiling] Indeed. In fact, the rampant media coverage of various scandals has fueled a cognitive bias in people, referred to as the availability heuristic, where they base the prediction of the frequency of an event occurring, like a person or company lying, on how readily an example can be brought to mind.

So people are conditioned to distrust?

Exactly. Today, everyone is subconsciously assuming that business people are guilty until proven innocent. Therefore, you should never believe that customers trust you more than they actually do. If you do, you won't take the steps necessary to monitor, develop, and nurture customer trust. And trust me, trust is critical in today's dynamic marketplace.

[Exec smiles] *I trust you, I think. And those steps are?*

There are many, such as demonstrating empathy and competence, becoming more transparent in your dealings with them, and eliminating buzzwords and corporate speak. Before we get to specifics, let's weave all five trends together and see what type of customer mindset evolves.

A confused and uneasy one, I'd suspect.

Rational man is a myth

Confusion is part of it, but not the interesting part. Gertrude Stein once remarked, *"Everyone gets so much information all day long that they lose their common sense."* This is precisely what has happened to today's customers. They simply cannot *rationally* cope with the overwhelming amount of choice, conflicting information, cognitive dissonance, and various influences, so they respond as people do who are under information overload.

The first thing that happens is they become frustrated. Let's take an example. Suppose that you want to buy your daughter a car to use to commute back and forth to college. You're looking for something reasonably priced that's also safe and gets decent gas mileage. So, where would you begin?

I'd probably start on the Internet.

Okay. You may begin by narrowing down your options from a mental short list of brands and models, but eventually you're going to dig a little deeper for information. And indeed, the majority of car buyers go online to research vehicles, and request information and quotes from sellers. So when you do your first Internet search, what do you imagine you're going to find? A few results?

A few hundred perhaps.

Sounds a little low, but okay. And will you look through all of them? Of course not. You'll become frustrated with the number of results and quickly limit your inquiries to a handful—perhaps the ones on the first page or two. And when you begin reviewing the information from those particular links, what do you think you'll find? Harmony? Consistency?

We've discussed this. I'm likely to encounter a lot of disparate information.

That's right. You'll discover that the data and opinions on everything from pricing, service, quality, and financing are all over the place. Some people will give a particular car a five-star rating, saying it's the best vehicle that they've ever owned, while others will trash it, comparing it to a bitter citrus fruit. Now, imagine for a moment how you'd be feeling while experiencing this information?

Like I said, confused and uneasy.

Right. First, you're frustrated, and then you're confused. So what do you imagine you would do next?

[Exec smiles] *Give up and move her into an apartment on campus?*

[Tom smiles] That may be the optimal choice.

What I'd probably do is narrow down the amount of information, based on what felt right to me. I'd probably also go out and drive a few and kick the tires.

So you'd ignore a lot of the information. You'd *choose* to be ignorant? Selective perception, right?

Excuse me?

I don't mean it in a derogatory way, but, in fact, wouldn't you be *choosing* to ignore a lot of the information?

Okay, I suppose so. But how am I supposed to make sense of it all? Assuming, of course, that it's even possible to look at all of it.

And there you have it! The nature of information overload is that you can *not* rationally deal with it and make sense of it all. So instead, you cope. But—and this is vital to our discussion—a funny, fourth thing also happens. Once you've "kicked the tires" and made your decision—a decision, mind you, that has moved through a progression of frustration, confusion, and ignorance—you'll become *over-*confident in it. You'll perceive it as being the *right* choice.

Overconfident? How does that make any sense?

It makes a lot of sense. How did you say you would cull information from the overwhelming amount that you'd be exposed to?

I said I'd select the information that seemed to make the most sense to me?

What you actually said was that you'd narrow down the information based on what "felt right" to you. Ultimately, your choice will be based upon that same thing. That one thing in which your faith has not waned a bit over the years, unlike your faith in just about everything and everyone else. The one thing that you know you can always trust.

Myself?

Exactly. Your instincts. Your gut. That's how you're hardwired—you, me, everyone. We reason with our guts in order to get by, as well as to feel good about ourselves and our decisions. Today's marketplace has forced customers to rely on that impulse more and more.

And that's why it's critical to understand the mind of today's customers? Because they're running on gut feelings?

Yes, and also because they unconsciously screen and distort information. But there's much more involved.

Two: Happy Now and Happy Life

All men seek happiness. This is without exception,
whatever different means they employ,
they all tend to this end.

Blaise Pascal

Tom: You really hit the proverbial nail on the head earlier when you said that you'd feel uneasy about your car decision.

Executive: How's that?

Uneasiness is the predominant feeling in the marketplace today. Customers are anxious about time, how to find more of it and whether they're using it wisely. They're anxious about money, how to make more, save more, and how not to run out. They're anxious about their relationships, how to choose them, improve them, and expand them. They're anxious about how to live so that they can be their happiest. They're anxious about their choices, both big and small.

But you said that customers are better informed.

They *are* better informed and more mature in their marketplace dealings. Customers are, in fact, in control of their "trips."

Not with the airlines.

[Tom smiling] That's a very good point. But you get my drift. Customers now decide what matters, how important it is, and how much it contributes to their marketplace decisions and to their lives. But with this control, in an extraordinary complicated stimulus environment like today's rapidly changing and complex marketplace, comes a basic instability and uncertainty; what to eat, what to drive, where to shop, what to wear, where to go, what to watch, whom to listen to, whom and what to believe, etc.

So, customers wanted control and now that they have it, they're losing control?

Paradoxical, isn't it? But you're right. And the pace of change is so brisk that consumers believe they must keep up with it to stay in control of it. They're afraid that they'll be somehow left behind if they slow down. It's as if they're driving at full speed on an unfamiliar, bumpy road, many with an overwhelmed, panicked look on their faces and others with a wide-eyed exhilaration. In any event, the landscape is pretty much a blur to them.

So how do we stand out in that type of environment?

Let's stay with the driving metaphor for a moment. Assuming that *you're* behind the wheel, and that you're in a hurry, what would attract *your* attention?

You mean, like a billboard?

In general, when have you found your attention shift away from the act of driving?

I'm never really focused on driving, per se. Unless, of course, I'm driving during hazardous conditions or on a challenging stretch of road. I'm typically in more of a trance-like state, listening to music or the news, running the impending day through my mind. You know.

Exactly. It's an automatic, subconscious behavior, like how you handle most other parts of your day. You probably commute the same route to work, stop in at the same coffee shop, grab the same newspaper, chat with the same people, check your emails, check out some familiar blogs, and so forth. We all do. The world of possible choices is simply too big for us to deal with, so we narrow our perspectives in order to feel safe and in control, and thus, get on with life.

Inertia is your enemy

Do you remember when, as a child, you'd wake up to a pristine, snow covered landscape? You'd rush out the door on your way to school, zigging and zagging, pushing and dragging your feet to create a one-of-a-kind, crooked path? Invariably, the next kid in the neighborhood would leave his home and follow your crooked path, kicking away more snow on his way, and then the next kid, and the next, until eventually there was a well-worn, precisely defined route all the way to school?

I remember it well. I grew up in the Midwest.

It's one of my favorite parts of the country. Well, that's what happens with your mind as well. It's easier, faster, and less risky to follow a defined path. You don't have to think or worry. That's why we're all, to one extent or another, creatures of habit. We have to be, or else we'd be overwhelmed with the countless decisions we're required to make each day. We make most decisions below our own level of conscious awareness.

We use shortcuts.

The crooked path is not really a shortcut. It's about involuntary movement along a well-known, comfortable route. If we think the same thoughts, or perform the same tasks over and over again, we develop neural pathways in our brains. Like dry paths in wet snow, they become paths of least resistance. We save a lot of time and energy by following these comfortable, subconscious routines.

We're cruising through most of our day on mental autopilot.

Exactly. And to break a habit or old way of thinking takes a focused effort. It requires that we *consciously* step out of our rut.

Something has to grab you. There has to be a good reason to step out.

Not necessarily. But it *is* true that something typically grabs your attention. So again, what would get yours if you were driving?

A lot of things. A road sign warning of some kind. An accident. A speed trap. Someone cuts me off or jumps out in front of me. An attractive person.

So, you're attracted to news and novelty, something that breaks the familiar pattern you're experiencing.

I may need the information. It may help me in some way.

Okay, you're filtering information to decide if it's relevant. Perception *is* selection, after all. And how does looking at an attractive person help you?

You're right. Sometimes I'm simply curious. I guess it's like listening to the radio. Sometimes I'm engaged in the programming or interested in the information, but at other times I may be bored and scanning the dial for something different.

You're scanning for information or entertainment that may help make your immediate future better. You're also looking for sensory stimulation. You want to keep your brain engaged. It enriches the trip and makes you happy in that moment.

I suppose that's it.

That *is* it, and it's also the major change in customers' priorities and preferences today. They're not only trading their time and money for products and services, they are also expecting happiness as an integral part of their experiences. They want to enrich *their* trips.

Through the benefits they receive from those products and services?

Beyond features and benefits

It's more than that. Of course, customers have always wanted to feel good about their purchase decisions. That's why they rationalize. But their desires and expectations have evolved over time.

Wait. What exactly do you mean by "they rationalize?"

Customers create various "reasons" to justify their decisions. In fact, human beings do this all the time, primarily subconsciously, in order to legitimize their actions and prevent feelings of inadequacy or guilt. Like me telling myself that it's okay to eat this dessert, because, after all, *you're* having dessert and I'll only be eating this one meal today. Things like that. And sometimes we even make things up in our minds after the fact; we fill in the blanks of our mental stories to have them make more sense to us and fit better with our overall story.

Anyway, at the turn of the 20TH century customers were choosing products based primarily on "features," like the quality and consistency of mass produced, packaged food, and they felt good about their choice of those demonstrably better products. Fifty years later, customers were purchasing the "benefits" of technological wonders like dish washers, washing machines, power lawn movers and TVs, and they felt good about the time saving and engagement they received from those products.

For the past fifty years or so, customers have walked the "hedonic treadmill," purchasing more and more stuff—stuff that marketers told them would make them happier still—and guess what? Even though their standard of living went up enormously during that time, they really haven't become that much happier. They have become much busier and more isolated, though.

An economist would say that customers have been experiencing decreasing marginal utility from their purchases of more and more stuff.

You're right. The whole notion that customers make "rational" decisions about what will provide "maximum utility" is erroneous. Sometimes their short-term behavior gets out of kilter with their longer term desires, like what has happened in our economy. Customers kept doing something past the point that it "worked," where it made them happy. And how did they adjust? They modified their subconscious marketplace value calculus from a *simple* equation—buy the best stuff at the best price that will do the best "job"—to a more nuanced, personal equation—buy the best stuff at the best price that will make me the happiest before, during and after the "transaction."

You're referring to the whole shopping *experience?*

Sure, today shopping is much more than a simple task-based fulfilling of wants and needs. For many, it's a leisure activity, as well as a form of achievement and personal expression. But I'm referring to something much more encompassing. The marketplace as a whole has become the primary place where people seek entertainment, where they socialize, play, discover and learn new things, contribute, and, ultimately, develop a sense of self and signal their identities. The places where people shop, as well as the things that they buy and the organizations with which they develop relationships, have taken on meaning far beyond their functional utilitarian benefits. And I'm not simply referring to "image-driven" categories like cosmetics, liquor, or fashion. Any product or service can be made more meaningful, even a lowly toilet brush.

I've seen ones that looked like they belong in the Museum of Modern Art. But I'm still not sure I'm following you. Are you suggesting that the role of business today is to make people happy? Do we even know what happiness is?

We have a pretty good understanding of what *creates* happiness. And yes, that's what I'm suggesting. And here's why: we've got enough stuff. We simply don't need another "whatever." If you want to grow a long-lasting, profitable enterprise, you have to create or own something both highly valuable and scarce. And in my mind, the most valuable *and* scarce thing is a strong brand protected by an organization with the unique capabilities to appeal to customers' changing priorities and preferences and ultimately, make them happy.

Okay, I have to challenge you here. During your talk last night, you said that no strategy can be more successful than the accuracy of its assumptions. You also said that customers express their true motives in their behavior; that what people do—what they choose—are their real priorities, not what they say. That said, how does your happiness assumption square with the fact that I do business with many people and organizations that bring me little, if any, happiness? As a matter of fact, some make me downright angry.

First, let me clarify what you think you heard me say. I said that customers express their *subconscious* motives in their behavior. This is a critical distinction. You continue to do business with those establishments because your *gut* is telling you that it's not worth the time and effort to change. You don't truly believe that stepping out of your rut will make much of a difference. In fact, it may take up some of your valuable time and contribute to your present level of stress. Many organizations count on that mental and physical inertia as their source of scarcity.

For example?

Well, do you frequent local establishments that you don't particularly enjoy all that much?

Sure.

So, why don't you walk or drive down the street and try different ones?

It's less convenient for me.

And that's my point. The fact that you're unwilling to drive a few blocks makes those locations scare resources on your particular subconscious, crooked path. But what if you have your interests aroused and subsequently focus your *conscious* attention on a *conscious* motive? Perhaps then you may *choose* to step out.

You see, the mind is like a machine that is constantly trying to predict how a change in behavior will make it feel, and it will only change when it believes that it will result in a happier future, both immediate and long-term. That's why customers are reluctant to change for a slight gain in "benefits." They simply can't equate that change with a happier life. Many people won't even accept a free product trial, because they don't like the thought of dealing with the hassle of opting out later.

People don't dislike change, not really. What they abhor is the unknown, because they can't *envision* it. They simply can't imagine how they will feel in *that* future. Customers are always imagining tomorrow, and a change could make tomorrow worse than expected. And they don't have the time to be wrong, nor do they want to kick themselves for making a bad decision. And that's why their past behavior is the most reliable predictor of peoples' future behavior.

So our goal is to make customers happy. *Okay, I'll bite. What makes customers happy, and how do we use that knowledge to both help them be happier, as well as improve our performance?*

Seeking happiness

The great Roman Emperor Marcus Aurelius wrote, *"Life is opinion."* I firmly believe in that sentiment. So I'm sure that everyone has a different opinion about what *specifically* contributes to happiness. That said, there does seem to be consensus about what *generally* makes people happy. And I'm talking about happiness while participating in today's modern marketplace, which is primarily an individualistic, do-it-yourself, and better-oneself pursuit.

First, let's make a distinction between near-term happiness and happiness in the more distant future. Let's assume for a moment that you love burgers and fries, which isn't much of a leap, considering how you've been attacking that plate.

Funny guy.

And let's also assume that you've just been diagnosed with dangerously high blood cholesterol.

Gee, thanks.

You're welcome. So now, when you go out for lunch and decide to forgo the double cheeseburger and curly fries and opt, instead, for the plain salad with balsamic vinaigrette, are you doing it to make yourself happy?

I suppose I'm doing it to avoid pain and suffering in the future.

Right, you're trading happiness now for happiness later. "Happy now" is the proverbial hamburger. It's about novelty and engagement, pleasurable sights, sounds, *tastes*, conversations, and experiences. "Happy life" is the salad. It's about improving yourself (mentally, physically, and spiritually).

It's about rituals and relationships, family and friends, learning new skills, growth, and giving back. So even though your impulsive self was telling you to order the burger, your more future-focused self won you over. We play that balancing of life choices game—happy now vs. happy life—all the time, moment by moment. The ultimate goal is to avoid the either-or paradox and satisfy the desires of both our happy now and happy life. Eat the hypothetical "good for you" hamburger, if you will.

So we should develop models that satisfy both selves? Isn't that the same thing as saying we should appeal to both the emotional and rational minds of the customer?

I don't really see it that way. I prefer to distinguish it in terms of the "thinking" dimension of the mind, which is very capable of making irrational decisions, and the "feeling" dimension, which at times is quite rational. The mind is like a small child walking a very big dog. The child—the thinking or "should" self—is the slower, weaker, more conscious part, which is trying to direct the faster and more powerful, automatic part of the brain—the feeling or "want" self. And it can do so quite successfully, especially if the dog—the "want" self—has been trained. But suppose a dangerous character swaggers out in front of them?

The child will be following the dog's lead.

That's right, and in fact, that may be the most appropriate course of action. You see, sometimes the more reflexive part of the brain—the feeling part—is more rational than the deliberative part. For example, when it senses that someone is untrustworthy and follows its gut despite all of the evidence to the contrary, it's making a "rational" feelings-driven decision. By the same token, there are many "happy now" desires that are quite rational, and many "happy life" ones that are not, and vice versa.

So that's a long way of saying, yes . . . appeal to both selves. That's what the very successful, LiveStrong brand did; it appealed to the "want-self's" desire to signal its identity, and the "should-self's" desire to help people. Ask yourself: how can I resolve the want-should, happy-now, happy-life conflict inherent in my customer's decision-making calculus? How can I appeal to the stressed out, impulsive, novelty-seeking, socially obsessed customer who also wants to satisfy his purpose-driven desire to better his future-self?

Like combining video with exercise equipment?

Hmm . . . yeah, like Nintendo's new Wii Fit gaming system. That's a good example. Thanks, I'll have to add that one to my list.

Don't mention it.

In a minute, I'm going to give you a model to use when thinking about how to improve your products, services and communication—which, by the way, means how to *add value* to them—along with some well-known marketplace examples. First, let's make sure that we're clear about this whole notion of happiness. Do you appreciate that happiness is primarily a cultural creation, and that in the developed world the marketplace is where most people go to experience it?

A cultural creation? How so?

You mentioned video displays on exercise equipment. Do people find happiness watching video?

Absolutely. The brain loves to be engaged. You said it yourself.

Good point. And do human beings find happiness pedaling a stationary bicycle or running on a treadmill?

I don't, but I know people who do. And your point is?

Think about it. Are human beings hardwired to experience happiness running in place?

I suppose not. But people certainly do.

They do *now*. It was invented. It's a cultural creation, just like most other things that people consider relevant and find pleasurable these days such as shopping, sports, video games, rock concerts, TV, movies, gambling, coffee shops, travel, jogging, and even Twittering. They're all more recent developments. Look at cell phones. We simply *must* have a cell phone today, right? And one equipped with a camera, calendar, calculator, games, photo album, and so on. Cripes, we wear them on our hips like six-shooters, because we may need it at any time.

Too funny.

But true. Now, consider my grandfather's way of life. He grew up, and grew old, in the outskirts of a tiny rural town, where he spent his days working his small farm from dawn to dusk. Happiness, to him and most others during that time, was rest and relaxation enlivened by nature, reading, and occasional social gatherings. You see, happiness was culturally determined then, just like it is today.

I think I see what you mean.

It's difficult to be consciously aware of our own cultural fantasies. We simply can't see ourselves, or much of the world we live in. In fact, that's why we laugh when comedians temporarily wake us from our trance-like state and remind us of the truth of our madness.

I once heard a comedian describe the "reality" of buying a hot dog at a baseball game— expensive, lukewarm, rubbery, soggy roll, surly vendor—and then he launched into a rant about how we tell ourselves how great it is: The picturesque park. The sound a fastball makes when it hits the catcher's mitt. The crack of the bat. The roar of the crowd! The beer! The hot dog! It's all wonderful!

[Exec smiles] *I see your point. It's a fantasy. We act out whatever we believe should make us happy.*

Strange but true. We have all escaped, to one extent or another, into the fantasies that we call custom, which is nothing more than humanly constructed and shared beliefs about the nature of reality and beliefs about meaning, value, and happiness. And while experiencing those fantasies, there's one particular theme that we seem to obsess over more than any other.

Let me guess: money?

I am what I choose

Money is a big one. Think about how we've hypnotized ourselves and confused the paper—the symbol of wealth—with the *real* wealth. We roll a shopping cart full of amazing foods from every corner of the world to the checkout counter, and feel depressed when the register tape prints and we have to give up $50 worth of "paper." We feel that we've lost fifty dollars. But think about it. We've got the real wealth in the cart. All we've parted with is paper. But, in our cultural fantasy, the paper is more valuable than the wealth because the paper represents power and potential, the opportunity for us to change our minds, whereas the wealth, the food or other goods, is simply a necessity.

That's true.

But there's a bigger fantasy than money, and it's our sense of self, who we think we are and where we think we belong. Again, the marketplace is nothing more than a cultural game, with the objective being to make us feel good about decisions, our experiences, and ourselves. Great brands understand, and help us achieve those goals.

Think about some of today's more popular brands. Starbucks works hard to make sure that customers feel special as they exchange pleasantries with their baristas, and urbane as they hurry down the sidewalk flaunting their overflowing shoulder bags and upscale logoed cups. Nike invests a lot so customers feel like winners, as they proudly tee up their $4 swoosh-embossed golf balls, despite the fact that they'll inevitably smash them into the woods. Harley doesn't sell motorcycles. It sells memberships to an exclusive club, where customers feel like rebels as they hang up their pinstripe suits and don $40 t-shirts, $300 pairs of boots and $400 black leather Harley jackets.

Are you implying that it's all about image?

No. In fact, it's just the opposite. Today the substance of a brand is as important, if not more so, than the sizzle in creating resonant associations and giving customers the subsequent "feeling." For example, when my friend picks her daughter up from school in her *tangibly* different Toyota Prius, she's telling herself and others, that she's a progressive parent.

So is it about keeping up with the Joneses then?

Not really. People don't choose out of rivalry with others. At least most don't. Instead, they choose what they do for their own pleasure and to enhance their *unique* identities and sense of worth. It's more about the debates they conduct within their own heads than a seeking of social status.

So people are not trying to stand out? Now I'm really confused.

Of course they are, but not by comparing themselves to their contemporaries and one-upping them through their purchases. Rather, they're defining themselves, as well as seeking meaning, security, and a sense of solidarity, by owning and experiencing *particular* things and experiences, and thus associating themselves with *particular* groups. It's how they affirm who they are, as well as how they signal their specialness to others.

So what they're really trying to do is fit in?

Right. People are not individuals, not really. They're nodes in a web of relationships. And it's through their various relationships that they reveal their "selves" to others. You know, I'm a Harley owner, a Red Sox fan, a Dunkin' Donuts guy, I shop at the farmers market, I own a Mac, I give blood, I watch the *The Sopranos*, I Twitter, and so on.

I don't know.

Don't believe me? Try buying a woman a pair of shoes that are obviously "not her," and then tell me what kind of reaction you get.

Of course. That's because others will see her wearing those shoes.

Her initial reaction has nothing to do with others seeing her in those shoes. She may never wear them. It's about how *she* sees herself. It's the voice in her head that also tells her things like, *"You're a caring mother,"* as she reaches for the organic eggs, and *"You're a fun mom,"* as she reaches for the whoopie pies, two minutes later.

Let me give you a personal example: Last year I was in Las Vegas giving a presentation. Prior to boarding my return flight, I wandered into a few airport gift shops. One was a Harley-Davidson store, where I seriously considered some of their branded merchandise as gifts. And get this! The retail prices of their t-shirts ranged from $24.99 to a whopping $222.99.

200 bucks for a t-shirt!

I know. I thought it was mislabeled, but was duly informed by a snooty employee that it was adorned in real crystals. Anyway, I decided to forgo that particular store and wandered into a nearby souvenir shop where the t-shirts sold for much less, something like *three* t-shirts for $24.99. The quality appeared comparable to the Harley shirts. After all, they were functionally equivalent; they were manufactured from the same material, in the same country, to the same general specifications. But I just couldn't get myself to buy one. Why do you suppose that was?

They were tacky?

The mind makes the meaning

Not really. The designs were tasteful. It had more to do with what I was telling myself *about* myself while considering that "deal?" It was all about the conversation I was having in my head. What "meaning" do you suppose I was creating? How about this: *"Well then. You certainly can't care very much for the people you're buying those for."* Or perhaps this: *"Boy. You certainly are one cheap son-of-a-gun."* Take your pick. You see, in the end it always comes down to what the purchase means to someone at the time of consideration. It's about the thoughts a potential customer or client is internalizing at a particular place and time.

Your t-shirt example appears to be about caring what others may think about you and your decision after you've made it. Let's take a different example: What could I possibly be telling myself about myself when I pull in to fill up at a gas station?

I don't buy your conclusion about the t-shirts, but let's go with your example. So, what are you filling up? A Prius or a Hummer?

Forget about the vehicle for a minute. What about the gasoline purchase?

It depends on the meaning you get from that particular gas station.

Like?

I don't know. Are you choosing it for the low price and

because you can run into the store and grab the paper and a cup of coffee thus saving yourself time and money? If so, then those functional aspects probably help you tell yourself—subconsciously—that you're smart. But what happens when the outlet down the street adds to that functional offering, such that you can fill your tank, as well as wash your car, drop off dry cleaning, grab lunch, mail a package, or buy tickets to the ball game?

I'd probably switch.

Perhaps. Now take a different scenario. What if you and others knew your particular brand of service station as the progressive, "green" brand? One that, with your involvement, supported various local, green social ventures. And what if you defined yourself as a "green" consumer? Would you switch because you could drop off your dry cleaning at a different service station?

I see your point. It wouldn't be as meaningful to me.

Listen, all I'm saying is that people are emotional, social creatures, so your organization should be strategically designed with that fact clearly in mind. Business isn't about numbers. It's about people and culture. The numbers simply tell you how well you did understanding and appealing to that culture. The fundamental notion that customers are rational actors, who are simply trying to optimize their individual marketplace choices, is defunct. Value can no longer be reduced to a simple relationship between benefits and price.

So why aren't more organizations working to add deeper levels of meaning to their offerings?

Most are lost in their own cultural fantasies and driven by self-interest. They're in that trance-like state that we discussed earlier—attending to to-do lists, emails, making presentations to analysts, worrying about paying for mortgages and private schools, hard selling customers, tweaking the numbers, and so forth. They're crawling all over the railroad tracks, looking for loose change and they don't see the train coming.

Others know that they need to change, but are simply whistling past the graveyard—preserving their status, and quashing healthy dialogue and the inevitable conflict and additional work that comes along with it. That's why this is so difficult to get across. It's not because it's intellectually complicated. It's not. It's because it's unfamiliar and challenging. Business people can't envision the happy now and happy later consequence of changing their *own* behavior. So, they resist change and let someone else deal with it.

So in essence, they're experiencing the same type of challenge that they're trying to solve with their potential customers— developing an understanding and a belief that a change will be "worth it."

I never thought about it that way, but you're absolutely right. Look, there are two types of change: change within a system of beliefs that stay the same, and change *in* your system of beliefs; e.g., your assumptions about the marketplace, your customers, and your role in their lives. If you want to change, you have to change twice. Yes, you must change the reality of the situation. But you must also change how you view that reality.

The business world is teeming with companies engaged in the first type of change. They continue to erode profitability and morale by changing within their old, ineffectual system of beliefs. A system of beliefs perpetuated, by the way, by many well-intentioned people and some not so well intentioned. So, you can either change within your system of beliefs; e.g., change logos, ad agencies, copy for direct mail and email. Or you can change your beliefs and then change *within* that *new* system of beliefs. Either way, you will eventually change your system of beliefs. It may simply take longer than necessary, cost more, and take a toll on your sense of humor and passion.

Remember this: When asked what single event was most helpful in developing his theory of relativity, Einstein is reported to have answered, *"Figuring out how to think about the problem."* People need to change how they *think* about their business challenges. In my view, they should think about their products, services, pricing, place of business, promotion, and people as a means to an end. And that end is to give customers a happy now, show them a happy future, and enhance their sense of worth and belonging.

Or develop something that customers can't find anywhere else.

That's what I just said.

[Exec smiles] *Touché.*

Three: The Balance of Value

*What the business thinks it produces is not of
first importance. What the consumer thinks he is buying,
what he considers "value" is decisive.*

Peter Drucker

Tom: So is this making sense to you? Do you
understand why you need a way of thinking that deals with
the reality of today, not one based on old assumptions? Do
you see the change in perspective that's required to succeed
in today's marketplace?

Executive: *Truthfully? I think I'm more
confused than ever.*

Look, you've simply become anchored. The ideas that
you've been exposed to about business, that it's all about
exchanging tangible benefits for money with rational people
who are trying to accomplish something in the marketplace,
is holding you down. You're habituated to it. You're stuck.
Your ideas about branding are also holding you down.
Branding is not about discovering your essence, nor is it a
graphic design and communication endeavor. It's about *creating* your essence by working *with* customers to uniquely
add value to their lives.

All I'm trying to do is share with you a certain attitude
and an insight that says, don't be fooled. There's a big
deception going on in the world of business, as well as the
business of non-profits—one that decouples marketplace
activities from the more meaningful aspects of life. Don't let
your habituated mind talk you out of the truth about the
marketplace.

Which is?

Aristotle believed that everything has a *telos*, which roughly means an aim or intention. For example, an acorn's telos is an oak tree. He also believed that human life has a telos, and that aim is happiness. Therefore, the telos of today's modern marketplace is happiness as well. Happiness that comes from a combination of novelty, social interaction, rituals, learning, and meaning. Happiness that is achieved by feeling good about ourselves, and good about our decisions and associations.

Our self-worth and identities.

Right. The evolving story that we tell ourselves *to* ourselves—the one that integrates our reconstructed past, our perceived present, and our imagined future. However here's the rub: Happiness must be your organization's intent. Not products. Not services. Not information. Not numbers. Happiness. Happiness is the customer's ultimate currency. It should be your context, the frame through which you view your purpose, activities, and results. Theodore Levitt's *"what business are you in?"* if you will. Your organization must be structured, and your people educated and inspired, to provide customers with happiness through its unique creation and execution of value—a.k.a. your brand.

Value! Okay, now we're getting to the heart of the matter.

I agree. But remember, I'm not talking about learning a new skill set or a new way of communicating some single-minded brand proposition. This is about mindset. If you're not "thinking about the problem" in the right way, nothing I tell your from here on out will make one bit of difference. You'll fall right back into your old "features and benefits," "unique value proposition," top-down, persuade via messaging modus operandi, instead of empathizing and collaborating with customers and innovating to add value and happiness to their lives.

I'm with you.

Are you? Do you understand the major shift that has taken place?

I think so.

A new map

Today's modern marketplace is about subjective well being, as opposed to material gain, and therefore customers are constantly on the lookout for better "value." They not only want the brands they choose to be reliable and fair, they also want them to look good, be good, and do good. Yes, they want to save time and money, but they also want to be uniquely acknowledged, involved, and engaged. To stay relevant, brands must evolve with customers' evolving concept of value. They must frequently reinvent themselves to stay fresh and uniquely add value to the brand experience. It requires vision, belief in collaborative innovation, empathy for the customer, and a passion for experimentation.

We are definitely experiencing a shifting landscape. I was reading the results of a survey the other day that showed that many people are even freely changing their religious affiliations to better meet their predilections.

It's certainly a chaotic environment and we are in uncharted territory, but it's not the landscape that's shifting. If your map doesn't agree with the ground, it's your *map* that's wrong. Do you see?

Sure. I get it.

And you understand what's required to attract these new, discerning and temporizing customers? You understand how to create something highly differentiated and desirable?

I believe so.

Okay, so now let's examine this notion of "value." Let's see if we're looking at it the same way. Define the word "value" for me, in the context of a marketplace transaction.

Well, I'd say that "value" is what something is worth to someone, the relative importance of it.

As compared with what?

What you have to give up to get it. Or compared with something similar, I guess.

Can you give me an example?

Sure. So, there are two competing banks. I choose to do business with the bank that offers me the highest rates, because that's what I "value" in a bank.

Perfect. Okay, let's say that tomorrow the other bank advertises a slightly higher rate than your present bank. Are you going to switch?

A slightly higher rate? How much higher?

What difference does it make? You just said that you base your banking decision on rates. That's what you said you "value."

True, but the difference has to be worth my time. And what assurances do I have that I'm going to continue to receive a higher rate? Plus . . .

Whoa, hold on a minute. Do you see what's happening here? When you gave your example, you were imagining *choosing* a bank. So, you pointed out the positive attribute that you considered "valuable," which was the higher rates. However, when you thought about switching banks, or more precisely, when you were *rejecting* the other bank, you started listing all of the negative attributes. Your gut feeling about your hypothetical situations conditioned your thinking, so that you ended up rationalizing *both* scenarios!

Which means?

Which means that you were unaware of precisely how

you were choosing and rejecting—your "value" equations. This happens all the time in the marketplace. Customers assess "value" in a complex, context-dependent, and, most often, subconscious and emotional way. For example, would you drive across town to save $50 on a $100 item?

Not with gas prices at this level.

Fine, would you drive across town to save $95 on a $100 item?

Okay, sure.

Thanks. Now, would you drive across town to save $95 on a $10,000 item?

Of course not. Why?

Think about it. Isn't the "value"—the cost-benefit ratio—exactly the same, a $95 saving for a trip across town?

Hmm. I guess you're right!

You see, "value" is not a rational, stable calculation. It's not some fixed "ratio" that you can plot on a graph. Yet, we can easily recite our company's well-defined "value proposition," can't we? And we become really frustrated and confused when customers don't buy into it.

True. Which tells us what?

It tells us that "value" is a relative concept. It "depends."

Customers simply don't think in absolutes like we imagine, or would like them to. Think about it. Customers don't sweat whether their mutual fund managers are keeping .5 or .6 percent of their investment, but they'll scour the Sunday paper for a coupon to save a few bucks on their next oil change.

And so?

So, the first step in creating something valuable for your audience is to think and feel what your audience is feeling. Don't judge them. Embrace their humanness, their "situations," and be close enough to them during those precise times when they're exposed to your types of products and services, evaluating options, receptive to messages, and making decisions, so that you can make informed predictions about how to stimulate their desire, have them care about and relate to you and your offering and, subsequently, make them happy.

Value is in the eyes of the beholder, and it changes based upon changing circumstances. Creating and delivering value is about figuring out how to "go deep" into your relationship with customers and their relationship with you, each other, and your brand. It's about new processes, new business models, new ways of thinking, new ways of seeing, and new ways of interacting. It's an endless game of innovation; of trial and error. The days of doing a little passive market research with customers, and then using that data to develop and launch products are long gone. Today, you must be immersed in your customers' changing lives, in their hearts and minds.

We engage our customers through a variety of methods, everything from online communities and customer councils, to soliciting feedback during product development.

That's great. It's smart to involve customers throughout the decision-making process. In fact, the customer should be at the center of *all* of your thinking and actions. But you need to understand their various social and cultural influences as well, at both their places of work and in their other "worlds." Remember, people do not make decisions in some kind of individual vacuum. We're social beings.

So we must stay tuned in to the countless social and cultural influences? Quite a task.

I agree. And we could spend our entire time together discussing various ways to go about it. But for right now, let's assume that you have your finger on the pulse of your audience, that you've immersed yourself fully in their "worlds" and feel what they feel, when and where they feel it. You've now got a simple, three step process to connect with them. One: use your awareness and empathy to create something highly differentiated and desirable—something "valuable." Two: attract their attention and interest—get them to stop and care about what you're doing. And three: creatively express and deliver real and compelling value to them over time.

Simple, huh?

Value is subjective

I said simple, not easy. So, let's start with step one. Let me introduce you to a model of value creation that takes into consideration the "who" and "what" of the marketplace that we've discussed. This first step is key; it's where you determine what's relevant, what's important, both for your customers *and* for you and your organization. This step informs what to be, what to do, and more importantly, what *not* to do. May I borrow a piece of paper?

Sure?

I'm going to take you quickly through a list of value components that brands use to innovate for their customers, ones they strategically weave into their thinking, organization, offerings, interactions and communication. The connection between your brand and your customers' happiness and sense of self is like this seesaw . . .

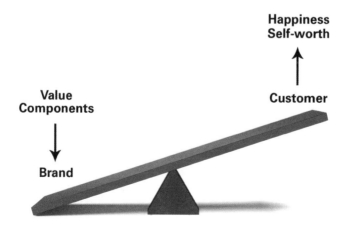

The more significant and meaningful value components you add to the brand experience, the higher it raises their level of happiness and sense of self-worth. Your goal is to lift your customers higher and higher by creatively adding more and stronger value components to your offerings, and this will increase their sense of trust and affiliation to your brand.

And different organizations employ different value components, and in different ways?

Every brand is unique, yes. But they are also similar in that they draw from the same list of components. There are no secret ingredients. Here's the list:

Conscience	Contribution, service, morality
Social	Connection, acceptance, attention, recognition, reputation
Growth	Creativity, learning, achievement
Involvement	Knowledge, control, participation, self-expression
Engagement	Surprise, laughs, inspiration
Aesthetic	Look and feel. "I like it. I'm like it."
Physical	Better-being, attractiveness, safety
Financial	Well-being, security
Time	Save time, make time
Performance	Comparable

Let's start at the bottom. Now, let me be clear about something up front: this list is *not* a hierarchy. The value components at the bottom are *not* subordinate to the ones at the top.

Like Maslow's.

Maslow got it wrong. In his world, there was no such thing as a "starving artist." You see, fundamental human needs are *not* hierarchical. But that's a discussion for another day. Just understand that it's the unique combination and, more importantly, the creative execution of the various components that determines success, not trying to provide each one on the list from the bottom up. Okay?

Sure. You know, it sounds a little like cooking.

How so?

Well, it's what great chefs do with their staff, and with the food and ingredients that makes all the difference.

That's a great analogy! So let's start with the first ingredient: performance. Now by performance, I mean those particular features and outcomes of your offering that customers consider the ante, the table stakes for similar products, services, and experiences. For example, it may be the storage capacity and speed of a device, how quickly a web page loads, delivery performance, gas mileage, rate of return, how quickly food is delivered, hours of operation, or ease of use and functionality. You may be able to stand out in the marketplace solely with this particular value component, but I highly doubt it.

Why is that?

Unless your performance advantage is truly "newsworthy," something that totally shifts your customers' outcome or experience paradigm, then it's simply one component that's ultimately factored into the total bundle of value. Remember, customers are skeptical of all of the superlatives tossed out by marketers—faster, cheaper, bigger, better, and so on—so what ever "it" is has to truly stand out. It has to be validated by the buzz in the media and in the marketplace. And, even if it *is* truly special, it's still only a temporary advantage. Others will quickly raise their performance standards to match it.

But many brands have been built around breakthrough performance advantages.

Of course they have. And let me be clear: I'm not telling you to stop investing in game-changing R&D to achieve a truly breakthrough performance advantage. I am saying, don't try to build and grow a brand around an *incremental* performance advantage. Most people simply don't care. All they really care about is that it's "in the ballpark," so that they can check performance off of their mental list and start factoring in other value components. Look, there is no objective "best" of anything. If there were, there would only be that *one* whatever it is. Right?

I guess you're right. To me, Google is the "best" search engine, but it still doesn't have 100 percent market share. Although its market lead is widening.

Exactly. Okay then, let's move on to the next component on the list: financial value.

You mean price?

No, not really. Looking at a product or service's price, yield, or rates is taking an inside-out view of a marketplace offering. Again, that's part of businesses' delusional view of value, that it's about the relative strength of *their* 4Ps or 5Ps or whatever the new list is as compared with competitive offers. Customers don't really care about price in any independent, objective way. They care about it as a component of the total bundle of value. If they value that "number" at all, what they really care about is saving money or making money. But even then, the money gained has no *intrinsic* value. It either represents future purchasing potential (happy life) or, in most cases, the emotional drive is simply the satisfaction of "getting a deal" (happy now through being smart or savvy).

But this is only true for products and services that lack a compelling *bundle* of value. That's when price becomes the main consideration, when all other benefits are just about equal. For example, let's say a customer is leaning toward choosing a particular product because it has a lower price, while having the same functionality as a rival product. The rational choice would be to buy the lower-priced product, right? Same functionality, lower price.

Right.

But, what if the customer gets a negative feeling from the

packaging? Or suppose the sales staff makes the customer feel unappreciated? You see, seemingly rational, simple choices are really complex, emotional ones.

So price is the determining factor only when all of the other value components are of relatively equal importance in the customer's eyes?

When the customer's expectation of receiving a similar bundle of value is present, yes. Or to put it another way: customers choose *comparable* products and services by *comparing* them with each other. They put on their analytical hats and use their conscious minds to evaluate the "facts"—like price—in an attempt to protect their interests and feel *smart*. But even then, mental disconnects exist, such as when people compare prices, but neglect to factor in shipping costs or other fees, or when popularity or competitive bidding creates preference and a corresponding, "irrational" price premium.

By contrast, customers choose things that they *care* about with their guts. They choose them for their *perceived* value, and to express their beliefs and ideals—their "truths." Your goal is to get customers to think with their guts and care, rather than think with their heads and compare.

Can you give me an example?

They're everywhere you look. From the clothes we buy to the cars we drive and the foods we consume, the price premium we pay is typically for something we consider "valuable," above and beyond its functional utility. How about that watch on your wrist? Or that cool notebook computer of yours?

Sure, but watches and portable electronics are luxury items.

They're luxury items today. It wasn't always that way. But okay, let's take a commodity. What about . . . say . . . produce?

Sure, but do me a favor and don't play the organic card.

Fine, I'll hold onto that one for a bit. Let's assume that I have two equal size bags of frozen vegetables that are the same variety, size, consistency, color, nutritional status, and freshness. Would you pay more for one bag than for the other?

Of course not.

Okay, but what if one brand enables you to steam the vegetables in the bag in your microwave oven?

Well, perhaps.

Time is more than money

If you value saving time enough to justify the small price premium, right? And this brings us to the third component: time value. But before we continue, I want you to understand something.

What's that?

We could spend all day discussing each one of these value components. For example, take businesses built around providing compelling financial value. A lot of new businesses are springing up that offer *free* products and services. Their revenues come from selling advertising in its various forms, or from affiliate commissions, premium services, sponsorships, or something else. And consider time value. Many companies are in business today simply to help people manage their choices, and thus their most scarce resource—time—more efficiently.

My intention right now is *not* to get into the details of various business models built around each value component. Rather, it's to make you aware of the different components, along with how you can bundle them to create something more compelling for your customers.

Okay, I understand.

Good, now the value of time is certainly increasing due to the pace of life and the amount of choice. Give me a few examples of how companies have bundled time value—saving time or making time—into their marketplace offerings.

Well, as you said earlier, examples are everywhere. Home delivery of everything from groceries and dry cleaning, to pizza and DVDs. My rental car company picks me up and drops me off at my office. Online shopping, banking, car registration, bill payment. Newspapers have introduced bite-sized dailies for folks who like to snack on media. The list goes on and on.

Snackable media. That's so true. Being time-starved and overloaded with options has lead to a kind of attention deficit in the marketplace. More and more people are multitasking and snacking, so as not to miss out. I've heard the condition referred to as continual partial attention and, as a result, you find everything from food and fitness to information and entertainment being packaged to appeal to this new customer reality. Considering that many people have more discretionary money than time, which makes time the more valuable currency, can you imagine how powerful it would be to combine financial value with time value in a marketplace offering, to save or make customers both money *and* time?

Absolutely! We have some industrial suppliers who do just that by handling certain internal processes for our company. And I suppose many online retailers accomplish the same with recommendations, product discounts, and free shipping.

Brick and mortar retailers do it too. Think about the big box discounters. Their balance of financial and time value works precisely that way in their customers' minds. *"For stuff that is 'good enough,' I can save a lot of money and time by shopping at a particular superstore or retail club."*

How do customers save time?

One-stop shopping for the basics, with no need to spend time scouring circulars and clipping coupons. The retailers' displays of trusted national brands act as cognitive heuristics, allowing customers to make dozens of annoying decisions without much consideration. When they finish, customers head off to their specialty retailers to pick up their more "valuable" items, like organic, free-range chicken wings, salon quality hair products, or designer jeans.

So in order to compete with a big box retailer, one would have to offer something special, something unique.

Right, a unique bundle of value. It doesn't necessarily have to be unique products; it could be a unique aesthetic environment or shopping experience. Let's keep going. The next value component is physical value. Other than the desire for safety and security, especially during fearful times, people are increasingly choosing products and services that they believe will provide them with "better-being." Not *well*-being, mind you. *Better*-being. They want to look *better*, feel *better*, and live *longer*.

So we're seeing an increase in everything from elective surgeries and various spa indulgences and fitness classes, to tooth whitening and anti-aging creams, nutritional supplements, organic this and that, and "enhanced" products like vitamin water and yogurt pretzels.

Krispy Kreme now offers whole wheat donuts.

Great! And we could wash them down with cups of fortified coffee! I've seen organic frozen French fries and natural Cheetos.

Funny, but I see your point. It sounds better, so it must be better. A few more cents for "better–being" and in the preferred context? Why the heck not?

Exactly. Reasoning with *feelings*, which brings me to one of the most powerful value components on the list: aesthetic and archetype. Think of it simply as the perceived value of the look and feel of an offering—from the design of the product and the retail environment, to the packaging, website, marketing communications, and even the celebrities and characters used in advertisements. If customers connect with "it," if "it" speaks to them, then it has value. The stronger and deeper the connection, the stronger the perceived value.

Are you talking about the brand's personality?

I like it. I'm like it

Personality, image, whatever you want to call the "feel" that a particular brand exudes. I like how Virginia Postrel defines aesthetic identity, *"I like that. I'm like that."* And that "feeling," that *je ne sais quoi,* influences many of our decisions without us being consciously aware of it.

Like the fact that we typically vote for politicians whom we like, versus voting for them based solely on their positions on the issues.

That's a good example. If we like someone, we require

less convincing about him and what he represents. That's what makes great salespeople such a valuable asset. They immediately convey excitement, caring, and competence. And the same is true of our marketplace choices. We don't choose a brand simply based on functionality, features, and benefits. We also take into strong consideration whether we like it or not, based upon how it looks, feels, and sounds. Companies like Harley-Davidson, Apple, Starbucks, and Nike have all grown their brands—their relationship with customers—by adding value to the intangible "feel" of their products, services, people, and environments. And so their customers have self-selected and created subgroups based on those aesthetics.

So again you seem to be advocating style over substance.

Not at all. I'm saying that the style *of* your substance is a source of added value. Look at the key difference between Wal-Mart and Target. Target strategically adds value to the shopping experience by emphasizing trend-forward aesthetics in everything it does—store design, merchandise selection, advertising, and so on. The company's way of *being* a discount retailer reflects more favorably on their particular audience's sense of self than Wal-Mart's.

Wait, advertising as aesthetic value?

Sure, primarily as a means of identity construction or enhancement. It can be overt, like the Apple "Mac vs. PC" ads and the Dove Real Beauty spots, or understated like

Target's, or like the style and wit of Bill Bernbach's brilliant "Think Small" ads for Volkswagen in the 1960s. If it's done well, if it matters to us and moves us, we'll associate with the idea and signal to ourselves and to others through our purchase, use and display of the brand, that we are "like that," part of a group that is fun, cool, irreverent, environmentally conscious, design savvy, rebellious, or whatever.

I'm a Tiger, because I buy Nike golf gear.

Right. But you don't "buy" the Tiger Woods and Buick association, because you don't believe that a multimillionaire athlete who is married to an underwear model would drive a Buick.

Ha! Okay, so it must be believable.

If you're trying to make a logical statement or connection, yes. For example, Nike's associations with Michael Jordan and Tiger Woods are sensible and powerful ways to bring its hero archetype to life. Otherwise, the value lies in the strength of the emotional association framed in terms of your audience's desires and sense of self and in the company's ability to inspire customers, make them smile, make them feel good about themselves and their association with the brand, like Aflac's duck and Geiko's gecko. Again, we could discuss this one concept for days.

Before you move on, would you consider quality part of aesthetic value?

Quality is communicated through aesthetics, although customers don't always understand exactly why. But yes, people can typically feel when a lot of care was put into designing and building something.

Let me leave you with this final thought to chew on: Recent studies have shown that people's *expectation* of how good an experience is going to be affects how much pleasure they believe they will experience *and*, subsequently, how much pleasure they actually derive from it. People's senses register even subtle cues in the look and feel of packaging, people, buildings, lighting, advertisements, and pricing, among other things, which not only affect how their brains *assess* value, but also how they actually *experience* value. Call it the aesthetic placebo effect. The brands, in actuality, take on the characteristics of the customers' expectations.

Wow! That's really interesting.

And incredibly powerful. You know, it always intrigues me how really smart people are surprised by the success of an offering that doesn't cost less or perform better, but is simply more aesthetically pleasing or more meaningful than competitive offerings. Aesthetics is a very powerful, yet often overlooked component of most marketplace offerings. Don't make the mistake of believing that since you can't objectively measure something, it has no value. As Einstein wrote, *"Not everything that counts can be measured. Not everything that can be measured counts."*

Engage or die

The next value component on the list is engagement. I'm sure you can appreciate the increasing popularity of things like music, sports, and video games. The amount of time people spend with online entertainment, especially video, is going to increase significantly over the next few years. Haven't you noticed the lines of people up and down the strip the past few days?

Yeah, I suppose gambling is simply another form of entertainment.

It sure isn't an investment vehicle. But it's not just about gambling. A lot of people come to Vegas for the spectacle, and for the shows and restaurants. Look, more and more, people are looking for laughs, good times, and surprise from the places they go and the brands they choose. And that includes the brands' marketing as well. Customers are looking to brighten their days through their varied experiences. All things being comparable, weaving those attributes into your offerings increases their value to customers. Think about your client conference that we just attended.

Very true. Our people did a great job making the past two days an entertaining and memorable event.

An event that enhanced your brand by adding value to your audience's lives. And do your people similarly make your advertising and training materials fun and entertaining, something memorable? And your retail experience? Is it interesting and engaging? And your salespeople? Are their presentations designed to move people? To inspire them, involve them, and make them happy?

If you start deconstructing popular marketplace experiences, and non-marketplace experiences for that matter, you'll begin to discover engagement value just about everywhere you look. Employees at retail outlets sing songs while custom mixing premium ice cream. Gigantic sporting goods stores are essentially adult theme parks. Hotels are adding everything from piano bars to indoor water parks.

I suppose you're right. I was channel surfing the other night and witnessed a financial adviser as showman on one channel, and a preacher as storyteller and comedian on the other.

Exactly. Look, there's no doubt that maintaining certain rituals strengthens bonds with customers. Customers want to trust in what they'll receive from a brand, so they can return to it without much thought. However, they also want the brands they choose to be interesting. They want novelty. For example, I'm pretty sure that those "shows" you watched use the same personalities, general themes, and set designs each time. But the producers are also creatively thinking about how to renew the "brand" and reawaken their audiences.

The marketplace is increasingly the place where people go to escape boredom, to be surprised and entertained, to laugh, learn, and become more engaged. So definitely weave those attributes into your brand, but just remember, just as teachers engage students for their students' benefit, you're engaging your customers for their benefit, not yours.

But what if we sell a boring commodity?

There's no such thing.

Huh?

Four: Identity and Community

Together we can do it yourself.

Slogan of a small town hardware store

Tom: There's really no such thing as a commodity product, only commodity thinking. Don't confuse an ordinary product with an ordinary experience. Anything can be made more engaging and meaningful. Wrap a comic strip around a piece of gum. Print inspiring quotes on coffee cups. Be a protagonist for something bigger than your products. Again, this requires a change in mindset from thinking about you and your brand (and what people think about you and your brand, and how to "sell" your brand) to obsessing over how to add more and more value to customers' lives and make them feel good about themselves and their decision to choose, associate with, and communicate through your brand.

Executive: *Enhance their trips.*

Exactly. Which brings us to the next value component: involvement. As we've discussed, today's customers are not the passive consumers of years past. They want to participate in the marketplace and express themselves. You can watch this trend manifesting itself in various technological advancements. People not only book their own travel and lodging, they also check themselves in at the airport, scan their groceries, manage their investment portfolios, bank online, and create everything from personal websites, music play lists, videos and books, to custom-designed computers, cars, t-shirts, and online newspapers.

These acts of *doing* bring meaning to customers' lives by allowing them to manage the things that matter to them, and thus strengthen their bond to the brand. In addition, their sense of having some control over their world makes them happy. Why do you think video games are such a booming business? We literally get a cognitive kick out of solving problems, mastering technology, and accomplishing tasks.

But you just said that we should be saving them time. Doesn't doing it for them help save them time?

Absolutely, save them time on activities that don't *matter* to them. I've even read about a business where customers could pay a small fee to have the first few *unchallenging* levels of their video game played for them.

That's wild!

The world is strange and wonderful. So, let me ask you: Did you use the self-check kiosk when you arrived at the airport?

Sure, why?

Well, is it faster for you to check in that way, or stand in line and have people do it for you?

But that's me. Some customers may want the assistance.

Then the company should provide the option. This value component is mainly about choice, knowledge, participation, and self-expression. You should give those who desire more information and control the means to get it, and give those who want to participate and express themselves, the means to do so. Brands today must innovate to enable customers to do for themselves, and thus create their *own* value.

With things like self-serve kiosks?

Sure. And search engines, store scanners, blogs, wikis, virtual worlds, online customer panels, custom websites, and social networks. The list is long and growing. Give customers the tools, information, training, and raw materials to do and create for themselves. I've seen high-tech grocery store kiosks where shoppers can choose from menu screens, such as healthy living and grilling, which then display beautiful photos of meals, along with the option of printing out a list of ingredients and recipes.

Listen, for now, don't get hung up on the various technologies and platforms. They're simply vehicles to use to add value to people's lives. Instead, know what's possible. And more importantly, understand the possibilities. Think about what customers may be saying to themselves about their experiences—"I wish I didn't have to . . ." or "I wish I could . . ." —and then use your unique knowledge, relationships, and technology to help them.

How do we find out exactly what customers want to be involved in?

A good first step would be to ask them. Also, look for

insights in their communication with you and with each other. But in many cases, realize that you'll only discover their unexpressed desires by observing them and walking in their shoes. Try to deeply sense what they desire and why. It offers invaluable information, letting you keep a step ahead of whatever will happen next. And remember, customers can't always imagine how to strategically create value through innovation. They can't see what's ahead around the bend. They're simply not aware of all of the possibilities and, therefore, will be unable to express or even signal their desires. That's your job. That's where your creativity comes into play.

For example?

Well, do you think any customer ever asked a toy store owner if she could build her own custom teddy bear from a bunch of parts? Or consider Nike's new running innovation, the Nike+, which allows customers to capture exercise data from sensors in their shoes to their Apple iPods. They can then sync the data and send it to a custom website, where they can analyze each run and stay in tune with their personal achievements.

That's pretty cool.

Yeah, and it even allows them to connect with other Nike+ customers to compare notes, or challenge them to a virtual race. Nike and Apple are also collaborating to make the iPod compatible with gym equipment. Notice though, how I referred to it as a *running* innovation and not a running *shoe* innovation. You see, innovation is not what companies do to their products and marketing. Rather, it's *how* they add value and happiness to customers' lives through their ingenuity, collaborations, and investments. To deepen your relationships with customers, to grow your brand and your business, you should continuously be asking yourself, how can we uniquely add value to people's lives—to surprise, enable, involve, empower, connect, and inspire them? Remember, this is your customers' time, not yours. You are a supporting player in their dramas—dramas that you help bring to life.

Value is what value does

Before you move onto the next value component, I have a quick question for you.

Shoot.

I was thinking some more about our client conference and, in addition to it being entertaining and engaging, our people provided a lot of "information value." I don't see that particular component on your value list. Am I missing something?

Where's the value?

Excuse me?

Where's the specific value in the information that your people provided? Look, I'm not trying to be disrespectful, but I hear that argument from marketers all the time, "*Our marketing communication is valuable because it informs people."* So it's easy for them to rationalize bombarding people with "information" in emails, ads, phone calls, direct mail, and sales calls in between trying to brainwash them with taglines and jingles. In fact, isn't information often likened to money? You've heard the expression, "a wealth of information?"

Sure.

Okay, in one way information *is* like money in that it doesn't possess any inherent value. Its value lies in what it can do for the recipient. But it's different from money in a very important way: information *consumes* time, attention, and emotion. Those are highly valued currencies today, because they're scarce. Perhaps that's why people say, "*Pay* attention," because they know you have to give it up.

Interesting. And based on the trends that you've described it appears that attention will be getting scarcer. Is that right?

Absolutely. And that's why information devoid of contextual relevance and meaning is disadvantageous. Time-starved people don't want more information. What they want is value—to gain specific knowledge, when, where, and how they want it, in order to enjoy it, connect with it, and improve some aspect of their lives. So as attention becomes scarcer and more valuable, customers will increasingly be on the lookout for a return on their attention investment. From a customer's viewpoint, a brand will become a proxy for value, an expectation of receiving a decent return on their attention.

So how do you think we did with the value of the information we provided? Did our attendees receive a decent R.O.A.?

Well, the information provided at your conference was *when* and *where* folks wanted to receive it. They did choose to be there after all. But what I'm trying to get across to you is that the information delivered wasn't valuable in and of itself. Rather it *provided* value, and in a few ways. First, as we've discussed, it provided engagement value. The information was packaged in a fun, entertaining, and inspiring way. It also added what I refer to as social value, which we'll talk about in a minute. And finally, it provided attendees with growth value, the next component on the list.

Wait, so information has value only to the extent that it adds value? What about the value of being exposed to something new, which may interest you but which you obviously need to be aware of first?

And what if that information is of absolutely no interest to me, when and where I'm exposed to it? Then isn't the communication worthless, or perhaps even a bother?

I suppose.

So find ways to weave value *into* the information, so that it becomes valuable.

For example?

Well, you did it with your conference, didn't you? Instead of emailing all of the event information in a static document, you brought your clients together to engage with, and learn from, each other. The information was also delivered in an inspiring way.

True.

So do that with every piece of information. For example, doesn't offering a free sample of something provide more value than simply broadcasting a message about that something? Or what if you delivered the information in a more contextually relevant manner, like what Google is trying to do with Adwords? Or, instead of simply announcing the release of a new offering, wouldn't customers find more value in a short, engaging demonstration, or in a useful utility or application?

Listen, the bottom line is this: Nothing you do is valuable, unless you can point to how it *adds* value to customers' lives. And please understand that we're just skimming the surface of the ocean of ideas here. Of course, a short piece of contextually relevant or compelling information that leads people to more and more value is perfectly okay. I'm simply trying to help you become a more strategic thinker about branding, customer experience design, and value creation, to introduce you to a new business and marketing construct that emphasizes the *delivery* of value, rather than the *communication* of value. It's up to you to use your creativity and intimate knowledge of your audience to uniquely bring these concepts to life. That's what gives you your edge.

By weaving in the various value components.

Right. Instead of trying to *stick* in their minds with clever communication, be a part of what sticks in their *lives*. Try to be where they are *when* they want to engage with you, or *when* they're in a particular state-of-mind, and design your business to add components of value to those real-life situations. Dig deep into their culture and create an experience that customers *want* to engage in and spend time with, or figure out how to save them time and deliver value as quickly as possible. Make sense?

Absolutely.

Help them achieve

So let's get back to your conference for a moment and talk about the next value component on the list: growth value. The information that your people provided was designed to help your attendees become more successful, correct?

We certainly hope so.

And besides transferring information and, hopefully, knowledge, what else did you do to add growth value, to facilitate creativity and learning. And I mean beyond mere participant interaction and engagement. I'm talking about having them learn new skills and leave with a sense of achievement. Think about how Nike+ customers can analyze their performance, interact with each other, and monitor progress.

I can't think of a thing, but I follow your point. I can imagine how one could weave growth value into a conference, through workshops and breakouts and by strategically connecting people for continuing dialogue and sharing. I even participated in an event recently, where attendees were given the opportunity to present to one another. But can we talk about growth value as a component of a product-oriented marketplace offering, say . . . at retail?

Sure. But for the record, I don't see marketplace offerings as "service" or "product" oriented. That distinction, like almost all distinctions, is a limiting one.

Sure, I understand.

So, let's take a supermarket, okay?

Perfect. So, what are you going to do to weave in growth value? Teach customers how to stock shelves?

[Tom smiling] Don't laugh too hard. Absurdity has been the catalyst for some of the world's most innovative ideas. I once made what I thought was a joke at a conference, saying that I was going to open a high-end restaurant where customers would be required to cook their own food. Some guy in the front row yelled back at me, *"We have one of those here!"*

That's pretty funny.

And it's true. That's my point. Now, think about what people may *enjoy* learning more about and getting better at, as it relates to a supermarket? What do supermarkets provide the "raw materials" for?

Cooking, I guess.

So what if a supermarket offered special evening programs focused on highly personalized, hands-on cooking classes?

Sure, but people are busy, remember?

Agreed. But what if the supermarket helped their busy customers prepare a week's worth of healthy meals, combining growth value with engagement value, time value, and physical value.

I see. And if they also saved them money, as compared with eating out or even making poor selections?

Now you're getting it! With this new model, you're shifting your thinking from selling your "what," to empathizing and creating a unique "how," how to add value and improve customer's lives. Customers are moving beyond being mere participants in the marketplace to being creators, collaborating and sharing aspects of their lives, their opinions, and their causes and passions. Success is all about figuring out how to tap into this very real desire.

Look, for an indication into the rising importance of growth value, simply observe consumer behavior. People are watching educational programs and how-to shows on everything from auto customization and furniture building, to home decorating and photography. They're taking sushi classes, participating in reading groups, brewing their own beer, and creating all kinds of art. Cooks and poker players are today's celebrities. So are photographers, designers, gamers, and computer programmers. If you can figure out how to use your brand to bring people together to learn, create, and share—perhaps by collaborating with *their* heroes and celebrities—your bond to them will grow stronger and stronger.

I read recently that quilt makers are a community that spends billions of dollars a year.

Incredible!

You know, you got me thinking about something. Our town recently hired a company to build a new community playground. The company acted more as a facilitator than a vendor. They brought all of the neighbors together to collaborate on the project, getting input from the adults and the children. They used local materials, volunteer laborers, and even incorporated local folklore and history into our design. It was an awesome experience.

That is a *great* example.

Take a look. I've got some wonderful photos on my iPhone.

Real life is other people

Very cool. Not many people carry around pictures of experiences they've had with businesses. That's a pretty good indication that you've received remarkable value, and a perfect segue into social value. You see, your iPhone and your photos enable this particular social interaction of ours. Therefore, they hold a kind of value: *social* value. Apple strategically weaves this value component into all of its offerings. And perhaps the playground company strategically provided you with social value as well, assuming it was smart enough to shoot the photos, format them, and send them to everyone in a way that could be easily shared, and that enhanced everyone's feelings and sense of self and belonging. Then the branded photos would *strategically* carry social value. Do you see?

And think about this: When we first bumped into each other, you mentioned seeing me at your conference. The conference, therefore, became the conversation starter, the social catalyst. Since there is obvious value in social connection—it engages us and makes us happy—your iPod, the photos, and the conference are all forms of social currency that you've used to create conversations and foster connections.

So companies purposefully try to give people social value?

Sure. When you walk into your favorite pub and shout *"Wassup!"* to your friends, you're using the social currency transferred to you by Anheuser Busch via its Budweiser advertising. American Idol is a huge hit, because its universal appeal gives a lot of disparate people social currency, something in common to discuss and debate. So do things like politics and sports. When you give people something to spark a conversation, share, and bond with or around, you're delivering social value. It's a fairly imperceptible, yet very powerful marketplace value component.

Are you're referring to buzz or word-of-mouth marketing? Like when I forward links to a funny online video, or tell my friends about a sale at a particular store?

That's part of it, but certainly not all of it. Strategically, you're after much more than a simple transaction or viral effect. You're looking for ways to continue to deliver value and stay engaged with your customers. You want people to *identify* with what they're sharing, to get emotionally involved and transfer those emotions to others. You're after something personal, enduring, and durable.

Remember, emotions are what motivate. They're what color our perceptions. We appraise the world based on how things make us feel about ourselves. And we also desperately want to belong. So the emotional exchange and shared context of the social currency should enhance people's sense of selves as well as their connectedness and their alikeness. That's the goal, anyway. Think about this. If a few people from your conference wandered over here right now, how would they connect with us?

[Exec smiling] *They'd probably do what I did. They'd mention the conference to signal their belonging to our very small, yet quite special, ad hoc community. But I'm not really following how one would creatively weave social value into an offering, beyond becoming popular and entering the zeitgeist, like American Idol or the iPod. Or by creating entertaining content, which people want to share.*

How did Apple weave social currency into the original iPod?

I'm not sure I'm following you. To me, the device became *the social currency.*

Right. But how did Apple do it? I'll tell you how: By selling culture, instead of electronics. By strategically differentiating the brand through the advertising, the tie-ins with artists like U2 and Lenny Kravitz, the design, the packaging. Everything was elegantly styled and expertly crafted to deliver a unique aesthetic value—a powerful and desirable feeling—that was reinforced by the experience of owning one (cool to look at and easy to control), and then transferred to others by the people who owned them. Think about the ads with the silhouetted, dancing hipsters. What stood out?

The white earbuds?

Right. The social currency.

So give customers objects that can signal ownership and enable social experiences?

Sure, objects, images, media, stories . . . *if* they're interested in being part of the club.

Club? What club?

The brand. The idea behind the brand and all of the people associated with that idea, that particular subculture.

And they're really signaling membership, more than ownership. They're identifying with the brand's unique aesthetic and point of view. And sometimes, it's the aesthetic that *is* the point of view.

Remember, the marketplace is as much about identity and community, as it is about stuff and money. Nearly all of our actions and interactions are in some way an expression of how we think about ourselves relative to how we think others like us feel and act in similar situations. So this isn't as simple as giving people the proverbial t-shirt to wear. They have to have an emotional connection to the meaning behind the t-shirt, as well as to the aesthetics of the t-shirt, and the other people wearing the t-shirt.

Think about that rubber band dangling from your wrist. The LiveStrong wristband isn't a *tchotchke*. It's the result of Lance Armstrong's strategic collaboration with Nike, which was perfectly executed; from the color yellow—the same as the color of the jersey worn by the leader of the Tour de France—to the visible endorsement by politicians, athletes and other celebrities. Wearing one not only signals charitable status and membership in the "club," it also gives people a way to start conversations and forge connections.

A cheap rubber band creates attention, acceptance, connection, and status. I've never thought of it like that before.

And it draws attention to what others are doing, enabling people to influence each other. Powerful, isn't it? Toyota accomplished the same thing with the design of its Prius. It makes you wonder why more organizations haven't figured this out. Anyway, if you look carefully you'll discover components of social value driving the popularity of everything from beer and footwear to bands and blogs.

Blogs?

Sure. Do you think people are reading blogs and interacting on social networking platforms simply for the information? Of course not. It gives them social value, something to talk about, a way to signal social status, a way to garner attention and recognition and to enhance their reputations. It provides them with the means to interact with each other, and feel accepted and good about themselves. I know people who check their stats compulsively. Their hearts swell when they add new "friends" to their networks, or when people post comments on their blogs.

So true. But social connections do drive a lot of information consumption and product purchases.

Absolutely. And they'll become more significant as the amount of choice and information multiplies, since recommendations from trusted sources help people reduce risk and saves them time.

Okay, so how would we go about weaving social value into our brand, in the online world?

There are many ways and, other than the common medium and the potential for increased reach and amplification, it's not really that much different than the offline world. Give people something fun, funny, or interesting to share with their family and friends. It could be valuable news, images, stories, or ideas. Remember, content will always matter most when it comes to social interaction. Even in the terrestrial world, if you're bored with your relationships, you will eventually move on to something new.

The bottom line is that we want our friends to be *interested* in us, but we also want them to be *interesting*. The same is true of the businesses we associate with and the places we frequent. Make sure to provide customers with rich, stimulating environments—ones where they're comfortable and can easily connect and interact with like-minded people and draw the attention of people they're interested in. Give them tools to use to express themselves and to share those expressions with others. Give them some "thing" that they can use to signal that they fit in or are "in the know," and badges that signify membership in that particular "club."

The idea is to figure out how to use your product, service, people, and marketing as *catalysts*, as a means for customers to start conversations, share valuable knowledge, and engage with each other, and as a means for them to signal their alikeness and bond as an exclusive, albeit temporary tribe. Your brand becomes the enabler.

Okay, but some things are inherently more interesting to talk about than others, like music, sports, television shows, and politics. Who the heck wants to talk about . . . I don't know . . . household products?

Be a protagonist

Right. And not long ago someone said the same thing about coffee and running shoes and cell phones. This is not about the "product." It's about the idea. The LiveStrong brand was not *about* cancer. It was about inspiring people to live life to its fullest. Dove's Campaign for Real Beauty is not *about* soap and moisturizers. It's about celebrating the natural beauty of *all* women and inspiring them to feel good about themselves. Even Kleenex went beyond tissues and elevated the conversation with their "Let it Out" campaign.

Yeah, I saw it. I don't know . . . Kleenex and catharsis?

Hey, you may be right. But think about it. When I was a kid, you'd have sounded like a lunatic if you suggested that a sneaker company could become a protagonist for grit, determination, and passion.

Okay, and if the company can't be a protagonist for something, or doesn't want to be?

Then it's not "feeling" hard enough. You heard me right. This isn't about "thinking" about how to get people talking. It's not about being clever and coming up with some new, whiz-bang piece of eye candy. It's about feeling and caring deeply about something that is important to people in their real lives. It's about doing something that's actually helpful, meaningful, and pleasurable. It's about having a point of view that customers want to connect with. It doesn't have to be earth shattering. It could be as simple as being fun and light-hearted about what you're providing.

The days of growing a business with a simple "make and sell" mentality, no matter how clever the marketing, are quickly coming to an end. Today, customers not only want the brands they choose to be of superior value (in their eyes), they also want them to be meaningful. So you must ask yourself, what is wrong with the world for our audience? Can we become a protagonist for something highly valued, something timeless, something bigger than us, something that they feel about our category that will improve their lives? And can we uniquely and consistently deliver a unique balance of value in a way that creates a strong feeling and *demonstrates* our passion and commitment to them.

And this, my friend, brings us to the final component on our value list: conscience value. As I mentioned earlier, customers want to feel good about themselves and their decisions. And lately, their collective consciousness has been raised regarding the plight of people and the planet. They're awash in news and stories about war, climate change, famine, and disease. Their lives are increasingly being touched by financial hardship, illness, natural disaster, and death. These images, stories and intimate, personal associations and experiences are creating a richer understanding about the fate of others and, thus, a deeper sense of empathy.

Customers relieve some of this sympathetic distress by buying environmentally and socially correct values in the brands they choose. We've already talked about the fact that people are not finding happiness in acquiring more and more things. Instead, they're seeking a sense of significance and meaning from their marketplace activities. They want to associate with companies that are doing good, so that they can feel good about themselves.

Well, "green" is definitely in fashion. Everywhere you look businesses are touting green products.

It's not a fad. Environmental and social consciousness will be defining elements of brands for years to come. And customers' morally sensitive behavior will extend beyond eco-friendly products. They'll make donations to various causes, choose products made by companies that are environmentally and socially responsible, and shop with retailers that have responsible practices. After they slip on their certified organic-cotton pants, they'll climb into their eco-friendly cars, suck down a cup of fair-trade certified coffee, stock up on environmentally friendly household products, and invest in socially responsible mutual funds. I've seen websites that rank all aspects of a company's social responsibility, from how they treat the environment and their employees to their record on human rights.

I've even read about Christians using the forty days of Lent to reduce their carbon footprints.

Well, customers' consciousness levels have certainly been raised. And they will continue to be, as they mature and are exposed to even more information, images, and ideas that stress social justice, connectedness and shared responsibility. This means that customers will be increasingly looking for a sense of contribution and service from their market-place choices, making conscience value a significant value component.

But remember, customers are also very suspicious; especially about these types of claims since everyone appears to be jumping on the bandwagon. So, it's very important to be clear about your environmentally and socially responsible initiatives, and to back everything up with evidence. Give customers the reasons *why* you're doing what you do. Make sure to be genuine and transparent. Let them peer into the soul of your brand. This is about much more than corporate responsibility and public image. This is about the essence of your brand. It's about caring deeply about what you do and how you do it, and connecting with people at a much more human and meaningful level.

So don't bother putting green lipstick on a pig.

Be calculating

[Tom smiling] Good one. In fact, any value component that you weave into your offering must be one that is embraced by the people in your organization, and embodied in their words and actions. Customers are always on the lookout for inconsistencies, not in creative executions mind you, which we'll discuss in a minute, but rather in "feel," intensity, and point of view. So everything you say and, more importantly, *do* must reinforce your story—your unique bundle of value—for it to be believable.

Be authentic.

Your *people* should be authentic, honest, straightforward and caring. But from the business, I'd say what consumers really want is a perfectly executed performance that provides them with a superior bundle of value for their time, attention, and money. Like theatergoers, they want to "get lost" in a fascinating, well-crafted, well executed, and passionate brand experience—one that is a perfectly attuned expression of *their* desires, sensibilities, and identities.

That's being a bit calculating, don't you think?

Absolutely! I think it's irresponsible *not* to be precise and calculating when creating a unique customer expectation and experience—a.k.a. a brand. But that doesn't mean that you have to be selfish and scheming. And there's a big difference between *being* calculating and *appearing* calculating. You want your people to be like skilled actors, musicians, or athletes, so that their unique personalities shine through at the right moments and in the right ways. It becomes second nature for them.

Look, I once met this great waiter who described his job to me this way, *"I'm not an order taker, I'm an experience maker."* Was he being sincere about his "role" as a professional server? You bet he was. Nevertheless, it was still a role—a role, by the way, which his customers enjoyed getting lost in *and* which allowed him to retain his own sense of self. Did he also understand the connection between his role as an experience maker and repeat business, making bigger tips, and so on? No doubt. And was his behavior consistent and calculating? You better believe it!

So please be other-focused and calculating when conceiving and growing your brand. Stay tuned in to the changing marketplace. Have fanatical attention to detail. Put your people at the heart of the brand, making sure that everyone understands his or her role in making the customer the star. And always, always put on a great show. A brand is a well-choreographed, dynamic performance, not a static promise. It's about arousing people's emotional drives over time through a unique expression of those evolving emotional drives.

Create a unique and compelling bundle of value, live and breathe the brand performance, stay tuned in to customers' changing desires, and they'll beat a path to our door.

Right, so long as they know your address.

Five: Different and Desirable

The single biggest problem in communication is
the illusion that it has taken place.

George Bernard Shaw

Executive: *Meaning?*

Tom: Meaning that before customers can experience your brand, they have to know it exists. And, as we've discussed, customers have evolved over time to tune out or hide from marketers and sales people. And yet businesses have not evolved with them. While the marketplace pendulum has swung from a fascination with image and consumption to a preoccupation with experience and value, business people continue to focus on exposure, awareness, reach and frequency, unaided recall, and other increasingly ineffectual concepts.

But you just said that they have to know about us. That's awareness!

True. But awareness is no longer an end goal; it's a means goal.

A means goal. A means to what?

Look, obviously customers have to be aware of you to do business with you. Your brand has to be in their choice set. The *non sequitur* is to assume that awareness *causes* sales. Connecting with today's customers and influencing their behavior is a much more demanding undertaking. It requires that you stand for something: *"I am this. I am not that. I believe in this. I do not believe in that."*

It also requires four key ways of "being:" being different, being desirable, being real, and being interesting. Being different gains your audience's attention. Being desirable gains their interest. Being real gains their trust, and being interesting gains their support. These ways of being will translate to things that you want your customers to say about you, to themselves and to others: "They're different. I'm really glad that they exist. I trust them. They care about me."

Wait, awareness doesn't cause sales?

I didn't say that it doesn't. I said to *assume* that awareness automatically leads to action is a stretch at best. It may, or it may not. There are a plethora of other variables to consider. But let me be clear: You can certainly spend money trying to spread awareness of your brand name, logo, and tagline and hope that when it comes time for customers to choose a product or service in your category, they choose yours. It may even work, especially if your brand is an impulse purchase, or in a low-involvement category. I once read a study that claimed that as a result of all of the media attention on NASA's landing on the surface of Mars, the candy bar maker Mars, Inc. experienced a short-term increase in sales of its Mars candy bar.

Strange. I suppose that's why politicians litter the landscape with signs. Overall, politics is low-involvement and a lot of selections are simply based on name recognition.

I agree. Most people vote primarily to feel involved and to avoid feelings of guilt. They're certainly not motivated to dig deeply into candidates' backgrounds and voting records. Most likely, the signs signal that the candidates are legitimate since they have the organization and funds required to get their names plastered all over the place. I'm sure that there are other cognitive processes involved as well, like social proof or the mere exposure effect.

The same probably holds true with advertising in other low-involvement categories, where habit is the primary drive and brand familiarity signals popularity or credibility. For example, suppose a private label battery is slightly less expensive than the brand name that you currently buy. Would you try it in your digital camera?

Why would I want to investigate or experiment with a product that costs a little less, but may not work as well? It's simply not worth my time.

Exactly. You're busy trying to cope in a complex world. Everyone is! That's why a lot of our choices are mindless defaults, the *"yeah, whatever,"* good enough ones. So considering that the marketplace is rapidly changing—media is fragmenting, people are increasingly tuning out commercial messages, search engine use is accelerating, word of mouth is amplified via the Internet, and brands are proliferating— wouldn't you want to improve your odds of connecting with these overwhelmed and busy customers, beyond relying on some kind of hit-or-miss, subconscious influence?

Absolutely.

Then instead of seeing awareness as an investment in mental manipulation, as an end in itself, view it as a means to creating attraction and delivering value. Raise awareness of your brand to a conscious, considered level.

Shift away from a top of mind, psychological perspective.

It's all psychology and sociology. What I'm saying is that you'll improve your odds of connecting with your audience if you influence at both the subconscious *and* conscious levels. Again, think of awareness as a way to attract customers and deliver value, and delivering value as a means to creating belief. And belief—creating an expectation with customers—is key, since belief leads to experience and experience leads to adoption.

If customers *believe* you can help them achieve their goals, look good, improve their relationships, feel good about themselves, and so forth, they'll take your call, stop by your place of business, click on your link, join your organization, or grab your product off the shelf. If they don't, they won't. As you made clear, people are simply too busy today to act on faith and take chances.

But most organizations are so focused on spreading awareness—of their mere existence or of some kind of static "information"—they've deluded themselves into believing that customers are easily manipulated, or that they follow some kind of linear, cognitive decision-making path. You know, awareness, information, desire and action.

A.I.D.A. Sure.

Desire precedes information

Well, it really doesn't work that way. We've already discussed the nature of *rationalizing* man. People rapidly screen stimuli and connect with what intrigues and appeals to them. Their attention may flitter from one shiny object to the next, but they'll only spend time investigating something if their guts, and especially their desire for value, have been aroused. Reverse the positions of the letters. It really works like this: Awareness, *Desire*, Information, Action. Do you see the difference?

Not really.

Well, I've been watching you for a while now, and you haven't even glanced over at that dessert menu. I'm pretty sure that you're *aware* of its existence.

Yes, but I'm not interested in dessert.

[Tom smiling] Right, because you don't *desire* dessert. But what if the waiter stimulated your desire by wheeling over a cartful of mouth-watering samples? Or what if the menu had enticed you to dig deeper through a more creative execution? Suppose our table was a huge video touch screen, which allowed us to view photos and ingredients, and watch video clips of the chef preparing the dish?

I see, and then I may be interested in learning more and perhaps trying something new.

Right. That's what great marketers and salespeople do best. They make you aware of, *and* stimulate your desire for, their offerings and subsequent information about those offerings. Yes, they put you at ease by being candid and transparent. And yes, they create a feeling of simpatico, which engenders trust. But more importantly, they immediately connect *their* offerings with *your* gut, with your emotions, desires, and beliefs. Now, most purchases of low-involvement products move from awareness to desire, then straight to action. Customers never even pause to consider their decisions. Their subconscious desires are stimulated by a feeling of liking, probably created by some form of advertising.

Look, most people believe in A.I.D.A., because it *feels* right. We *feel* that it works like this: We sense something in the environment—be it some form of marketing communication, retail outlet, product, or salesperson—which then causes us to *think* about that something. Then, after thinking about it for a bit, we develop a feeling about it. And that subsequent feeling is what drives some type of action. Right?

That makes perfect sense to me.

It does to most people. So let's walk through a hypothetical situation. Suppose you're walking down a country road near your home, when you come across an empty produce cart. Leaning against the cart is an old board with the words "fresh farm eggs. $1 a dozen" hand painted on it. Now, assuming that you really like eggs, take me through the mental process that you'd go through to decide to purchase those eggs. Go ahead. You sense the sign . . . awareness . . .

Okay, I become aware of the sign; I sense it. I then read the message and think about its relevance to me. I like eggs . . . a lot. These eggs are farm fresh, which means that they're probably organic. I'm also supporting a local farmer. The eggs are probably fresher than the ones I usually buy at the supermarket. And the price is even a bit cheaper. I feel good about all of this, so I'll probably buy the eggs.

Perfect. Now, let's change the scenario. Same country road. Same cart. Same wooden sign. But this time, the hand painted message is "free flying lessons." You've always wanted to learn how to fly, and you have a lot of spare time on your hands. So, go ahead. You sense the sign . . .

Are you kidding? I sense the sign and wonder what kind of nut painted it and why.

You had a strong gut reaction to that sign.

I certainly didn't have to think about it.

Exactly. You sensed the sign and immediately discounted the message. You didn't really think much about it at all. That's how the brain works. You sense something and automatically have a feeling about it. This gut feeling is fast, effortless, and associative. It's also typically below your own level of conscious awareness. You then decide, based on said feeling and in many cases subconsciously, whether or not to invest more of your time in it and attention to it. Whether to raise it to a conscious, deductive reasoning process, like you did with the eggs.

What do you mean by "associative?" What did I associate the sign with?

The mind makes the meaning

Pass me a piece of paper, will you? Take a look at this:

cna yuo raed thsi?

Sure, I can read it. Why do you ask?

Remember how we talked about how the mind makes meaning out of partial information? Like the triangle folded in the toilet paper?

Yeah, I remember.

Well, you just made meaning out of a bunch of jumbled letters. You accessed your memory and, based on what was happening at the moment, on the context, your mind re-arranged the letters to make "sense." So what's this?

I have no idea.

Okay, now what is it? Draw what comes next.

It looks like the letter H. Okay, here you go

Right, because again, your mind detected a pattern and made a prediction in order to make meaning. It made a guess as to what I drew—the letter H—as well as what should come next—the letter E. Okay, so what comes after this?

TAE CA

I suppose this.

TAE CAT

Now really think about that for a moment. Do you see what you just did?

It's interesting, but what does any of this have to do with my question? What association was I making with the sign?

Just look at what you did: You took a meaningless symbol and "associated it" with both the letters H *and* A. How could it possibly be both?

It works based on what you wrote down.

It "makes sense" based on what I drew. You made predictions and associations based on the context. And based on the context of the "free flying lessons" sign, you associated the message with . . . what did you say? A nut?

[Exec smiling] *Perhaps a little harsh.*

Whatever your particular feeling was, it then caused you to make some kind of subconscious prediction about the future. And that prediction triggered a little voice in your head that said, don't think about it for another second.

You see, both signs captured your attention, which is the critical first step in any kind of transaction or relationship. But you made very different assumptions about those messages and about the message writer—assumptions that either created attraction and moved your mind forward or stopped it dead in its tracks. Even though both messages may have been honest and well-intentioned, your "truth" about them was very different.

My truth?

Focus on their truth

Right. Your perception, your interpretation. You have no idea at all about the "facts"—the reality—of either message. Instead, *you* made the meaning—your truth—out of what little bit you hastily perceived. This is the nature of perception. Small, and sometimes apparently insignificant, contextual details can have an automatic effect on feelings, thoughts, and actions.

In his book *Story*, the legendary screenwriter Robert McKee wrote, *"What happens is fact, not truth. Truth is what we think about what happens."* Facts are reality; for example, smaller cars are safer than SUVs. But truth is perception; bigger is safer, right? Facts are the way things are; for example, it doesn't matter what golf ball I hit, it's still going to end up in the woods. But truth is the way my brain views things; my thoughts, opinions, evaluations, feelings, and conclusions: I'm a winner . . . like Tiger. So I need a ball with a swoosh on it. We believe that our truths *are* the facts.

I'm a little confused.

This is a difficult concept to grasp. Not because it's intellectually challenging; it's not. Rather, because it's difficult to *feel*. For example, do you feel that you are the outgrowth of a spinning sphere that is rocketing through space at more than twenty times the speed of a bullet?

The Earth is traveling that fast!?

It sounds impossible, doesn't it? How about the two valley girls chatting on the beach one night. One girl asks, *"Which do you think is farther away, the moon or Italy."* To which her friend replies, matter-of-factly, *"Duh? Italy. You can see the moon."*

Pretty funny. And what does all of this have to do with marketplace success?

Your customers and potential customers judge you based upon the very little bit of you that they perceive, whether it's the facts or not. So everything that they perceive matters—and I mean every little thing— because they speed read you (pattern recognition) and prejudge you with their resultant feelings (categorization), just like you did with those two signs.

Everything?

Yes, everything that customers experience, which they can then use to make a prediction about you and your offerings. Great brands choreograph all of the little details. As the story goes, Conrad Hilton, the founder of Hilton Hotels, was asked at a celebration of his life for the single, most important lesson he'd learned during his long and successful career. He replied, *"Remember to tuck the shower curtain inside the bathtub."*

How true. It's the little things that can really make a big difference.

Exactly. Walt Disney once said, *"Whenever I go on a ride, I'm always thinking of what's wrong with the thing and how it can be improved."* But what do most organizations do to address this customer reality, to influence their perceptions and behavior? They ignore the customers' empirical "data"—the experiential look and feel—and instead work like hell on the secondhand, semantic data. They try to persuade people with all of their clever reasons, facts, specs, studies, and so forth. But the *facts* business, the persuasion business, is out of date. Instead, they should be working to understand and appeal to people's *truth*, because perception conditions people's sensibilities and their subsequent actions. And action is the business everyone is really in.

But the facts certainly matter, right?

[Tom smiling] Of course they matter. But only the ones that your customers are interested in, and only when they're interested in them. If you walked into an auto dealership and expressed interest in a classic red, convertible sports car, would you want the salesperson to start rattling off 0–60 mph figures and nuances of on-the-limit handling?

Huh? No, certainly not.

Right, because if he or she did, you may get confused and walk away. Look, being different, appealing to people's feelings and innate curiosity is like warming up a cold audience. You're looking for ways to appeal to easily distracted people, people with a lot of disparate thoughts flowing through their minds. You're trying to kindle their interests, and carefully move their thoughts to involvement with you. Later, they may choose to extract more information to validate that interest and perhaps gain more value through conscious, rational participation. But that'll happen *after* they've sold themselves by experiencing the look and feel of you and your offerings.

When they do seek out more detail, make sure that your facts are easy to find, easy to understand, and based on what matters to them; make the experience enjoyable and easy to share with others. But don't waste your time and money trying to persuade people with those facts. You motivate through emotion and then allow people to persuade themselves, to walk themselves through the process of answering the unanswered questions. Be obsessed with your audience's truth, and design your business to appeal to that truth. Let the design of your products, facilities, marketing, and interactions be a cue to your unique bundle of value.

Okay, let me see if I'm following this. Being different is the crucial first step, and it should be designed to capture customers' attention, stimulate their interest, and strategically help shape their perceptions.

Exactly. To create attraction. Attraction is a process, not an end. You're staying tuned into people's changing lives, and attracting them in order to take them where they want to go, where you can add value to their lives. So you want to be different in a way that connects with customers' beliefs and desire for value. Appeal to your audience's sense of self and self-interests. And when I say different, I mean different with a capital D! Otherwise, their busy brains will "recognize" the stimulus, categorize it, make a quick prediction about it, and then probably tune it out. You want to *violate* their expectations, what they think they know about your brand, and engage their conscious attention.

Your how is your edge

Look, in simpler times with fewer products and top-down control of communication, a more rational, semantic approach was *de rigueur;* marketers discovered unfilled competitive niches, developed dogmatic comparative slogans, and invested heavily in "talking to us," all in an attempt to "burn" their positions into our minds. *"We try* harder." "Quality is job one." "You're in good hands." "A chicken in every pot. A car in every garage." As we've discussed, it was a pretty basic era comprised of naïve people who responded to a basic branding process—shape perceptions through simpleminded, repetitive communications.

Today's is a much different world. We buy our chickens in a bucket, on a bun, as a fajita, from General Tso, free-range, frozen, fresh, or fried. And don't even get me started on cars, trucks, vans, SUVs, gas, diesel, electric, hybrid, and solar powered. The amount of vehicle choice is approaching Starbucks-like proportions. The marketplace is teeming with products and services all making similar comparative and superlative claims.

But take a close look at some of today's most *effective* marketing and see if you can discover the unique "positions" (a.k.a. overt benefits). From Apple's information bereft advertising and packaging, to Aflac's duck and Geico's cavemen, to McDonald's revamped menus and refurbished restaurants, marketing has changed. And for a very simple reason . . .

Yeah, people are sick and tired of all of the mind-dulling repetition and uninspiring messages: "We're bigger, cleaner, faster, whiter, and brighter." *How can everyone be the "best?" It doesn't help improve our lives; it just adds to the confusion.*

That's exactly right. Organizations are wasting money today trying to impress people or pound one big brand idea into their heads. It's tedious and, frankly, it appears desperate and out of touch. And remember, the marketplace is no longer merely a means to an end, where we compare, contrast, and attempt to optimize our purchases and get on with our lives. It is now a major part of our lives. We expect the marketplace to surprise and delight us, and we want our choices to reflect favorably on our various, and eclectic, senses of selves. Instead of being directed, we want to discover, uncover, and intuit the role a product or service might play in making us happy and helping us become more of who we want to become.

So, marketing is evolving.

Exactly. Astute marketers are now aware that rational man is a myth, and that we live in a skeptical, postmodern marketplace. A marketplace that bores easily, trusts little, and is sick to death of authoritative messages, no matter how subtle.

Thus, the strategic appeal to customers' feelings.

Right. Formality, serious-mindedness, and left-brained, rational and unambiguous messaging are giving way to humor, drama, irony, and inspiration. The emphasis is shifting from "what" a company does, to "how" it does it. The "what" is about logic and thinking, conveying structured and precise *semantic* information designed to impress, persuade, and convince people. The "how" is about creativity and feelings—emotional, untidy, and aesthetically appealing sights and sounds designed to attract and charm, and create desire, curiosity, and conversations. Today it's all about *pragmatic* meaning; the truth that customers make for *themselves* about what the brand is about, and why it says and does what it does.

[Exec smiling] *First facts vs. truth, and now what vs. how? Damn, this is getting confusing.*

[Tom smiling] Just different than what you're used to, that's all. Think of it this way: The great film critic Roger Ebert once remarked, *"A movie is not about what it is about. It is about how it is about it."* The movie *Field of Dreams* is about what?

Baseball.

Right? But so is *The Natural*. And so are *The Bad News Bears* and *Angels in the Outfield*. And *Bull Durham* and *Major League*.

Don't forget Fever Pitch.

[Tom smiling] Oh . . . a member of Red Sox Nation, are we? But do you see my point. *What* you do isn't what's most important today. A lot of organizations do *what* you do. What matters is *how* you do it, how you bring it to life for the benefit of your customers and employees. Being different today is much more important than being better.

Again, take a good look at today's most popular and talked about brands, and what you'll find are very clear differences in their essences—who they are and why they do what they do—which is revealed in the design of their products, processes, people, environments, and communication. You'll also find a big difference in how they approach the world. They don't pander or push. They play hard to get. They entice people to discover, dig deep, question, construct, and share. They're constantly coming up with ideas that convey their brand's empathetic, spin-free, and very human nature. Ideas that seduce, not sell. Ideas that communicate, *"I'm like you,"* not *"You need me."* They're not positioning conformists who try to plug into the intellect. They're passionate non-conformists who tickle people's emotions. They engage people and get them to tune out their comparing minds, and tune in their desire for discovery, meaning, and for a happier life.

So communicate our difference?

Communicate *with* difference! You don't want anything you do to look or feel like marketing or messaging. In fact, resist the urge to "talk," and instead innovate to improve people's lives. As Elvis so passionately put it: *"A little less conversation, a little more action please."* That way it won't be rejected at the outset. Again, look at every single touch point, every moment of the customer's "truth," as an opportunity to deliver value.

And what are the best ways to do that? Do you have any examples?

Nobody knows anything

You do it by being a protagonist for something bigger than your "what;" something that will improve people's lives. And yes, I've got plenty of examples. But look, an organization's "how" is its unique, strategic advantage. Like the execution of those baseball movies, it's what makes them special. It's impossible for me to give you a generic marketplace success "formula." In fact, William McElcheran wrote, *"For the mystic what is how. For the craftsman how is what. For the artist what and how are one."*

What? Look, there must be a process?

[Tom smiling] Whenever I'm asked that question, I'm reminded of a line from a book of tips and stories about successful script writing by William Goldman called *Adventures in the Screen Trade.* Here was a guy who, at the time of the book's publication, had written the screenplays for such critically acclaimed movies as *All the President's Men* and *Butch Cassidy and the Sundance Kid.* He certainly understood the "formula" for Hollywood success, right? But what three-word insight from that book is he most well-known for? *"Nobody knows anything."*

I've read that, but I never knew the origin. Okay, but surely there are executions that you'd consider exemplars.

Of course, but remember I'm trying to provide you with a framework—a set of assumptions and concepts that constitute a way of viewing reality and a way of *being*—not a recipe or prescription. It's a framework that emphasizes the delivery of value over the communication of information. As soon as someone gives you a formula, you have *his* reality filtered through *his* mind, which, again, is a limiting view.

Sure, I understand.

Well, one example that comes to mind is something I read about the European mobile phone operator Orange. A few years ago, at the Glastonbury Festival in England, Orange released an innovative *Text Me Home* tent to improve the festival life of concertgoers. When the receiver in the tent was sent a text message, it triggered an antenna to rise and light up as an orange beacon, so that users could find their tents when stumbling back to them in the dark.

That's really cool.

Indeed, but do you appreciate the shift in perspective? Instead of passing out flyers or promotional offers to tens of thousands of people, Orange created something unique, valuable and newsworthy. It got close to its audience, and then interacted and engaged them with something that mattered right then and there, in their real lives. That's the key to marketing and sales success today: Be there when and where your audience's need is the greatest, and then introduce compelling value into their existing habits and routines. Do things of value that connect to your brand, and that people will remember and talk about. And it really doesn't matter how sexy your "what" is. Is there free WiFi here?

I believe so. Let me try to go online . . . okay . . . I'm on.

Great. Go to www.brewsomegood.com and take a look at what Maxwell House is doing.

"Here's to a world without bitterness."

Right, they're celebrating optimism. Maxwell House has become a proponent for smiling, for sharing some good news in an increasingly cynical world of bad news. And it's trying to associate this value, this attempt to create some positive change and make people happier and more alive, with its brand in a creative and useful way.

I see. It's about more than the coffee, but the coffee is the lead actor.

Actually, the customer is always the lead actor. What the company is trying to do is weave people into that particular story, into that experience *with* the brand. Remember, people are creatures of habit. In fact, more so than you're probably even aware. A recent study found that most people hardly ever leave the vicinity of their home or office, remaining within a 20-mile radius almost all the time. They visit the same places over and over. You want to figure out how to add value to those routines, to become part of those places—real and virtual. You want to have people store in their memories the fact that your brand has provided value and enhanced their identities. Then, they'll come back to you for more, again and again.

Not as easy as it sounds, I'm sure. So what companies would you view as role models in effective sales and marketing?

There's a handful doing it right, but in my opinion none as effectively as Apple. The company is always innovating to add value to the customer's experience. And its marketing is culturally relevant, eloquent and entertaining, and does a great job of focusing on the customer's identity and experience, and bringing it to life. And Apple's attention to every detail of the product and retail experience is exemplary. I heard that it even hired particular hand models to make the iPhone *appear* smaller in advertisements.

Incredible, and quite calculating.

So I'd say be *like* Apple, and ask these kinds of questions: How can we differentiate ourselves and harness "feel" in everything we do to create curiosity and uniquely demonstrate our brand? How can we creatively demonstrate our brand, while encouraging interactions between people so that they influence each other? How do we continuously create energy and word-of-mouth through specific actions that will add value to our customers' lives?

Look at everything you create, from advertising and store design to microsites and packaging and ask: Does this cause people to stop and look and listen? Is it unexpected *and* desirable? Is it completely different than what they've come to expect from brands in our category, as well as from the medium? Does it powerfully tap into their desired sense of self and transfer the feeling of adoption and ownership? Does it fit their lifestyle? Does it demonstrate value at an empirical level? Is it newsworthy? Would people tell others about it, and why? People are looking for ways to quickly weed out the plethora of choices, so provide them with something that they can connect with.

So let me see if I've got this straight: Being different means that the product or experience should violate people's expecta-

tions so that they engage with it at a conscious level. It should also be a cue to the inherent value of the brand. And being desirable means that it should deliver value, be meaningful, and memorable. Is that right?

That's a great summary. And remember, you want that memory to be a vivid one, one raised to a heightened conscious level. You also want it to be newsworthy, to be a statement of who you are and how you are different. Let the press and your customers tell your story. And finally, try to connect people to each other in some way. Experiences with others are lasting memories that customers can relive over and over again.

Ask yourself: How can we elicit belief through actions? When HSBC—*"The world's local bank"*—wanted to bring its brand to life in New York City, it wrapped a cab in its company colors, drove the streets of New York, and offered free rides to its existing customers.

Wow!

Exactly! Go for wow! Don't say, *"Just Do It,"* do it with them! Don't tell them that you can save them time, work with them and save them time! Don't tell them that you want to be their friend, be their friend! If customers experience with you, and with each other, they'll come to believe. And belief is the path to action.

Six: Real and Interesting

Who are you going to believe, me or your own eyes?

Chico Marx

Executive: *Okay, we're different and desirable. We have our audience's attention and interest. Isn't marketing's job done at this point?*

Tom: Sure, in low-involvement situations or for low-involvement products, where trust is gained primarily through familiarity, and where the relationship is more utilitarian and transactional. Otherwise, your work has just begun. Connecting on a deeper and more meaningful level with today's discerning customers is not as simple as categorizing them, and then simplemindedly appealing to their motivations. People's eyes glaze over when their complex lives are dumbed down to some stereotypical image or marketing pitch. In order to truly connect, the organization or the brand needs to be as complex and real as its customers. Being real is what gains you their trust, and being complex and interesting gains their affinity and ongoing support.

Because customers want to see themselves reflected in the brand?

They want to see their *idealized* selves, the real, complex and interesting ones. So let's talk about being real and gaining trust. How do you determine whom, or what, to trust, considering the fact that you're similar to most people and therefore probably don't trust businesses or the people who run them?

Well, as we've discussed, I'd probably intuit trust based upon everything that I've seen, heard, and read.

And what, precisely, are you intuiting?

Whether or not my expectations will be met, I suppose. Whether the person or product or service will deliver what it promises to deliver?

Okay. But what if you've just met a salesperson and haven't even begun to discuss specific desires and expectations? Or perhaps you're driving past some restaurants looking for a place to eat, or looking at a few websites trying to decide which companies to research further.

I see your point. Well, I suppose that after whatever it is has gained my attention and stimulated my desire, I'll try to quickly determine whether it, and the organization behind it, is competent, honest, and caring. Does it come across as passionate and a confident advocate for the value that it's offering?

So you're basing your assessment on your perceptions, like you did with the hypothetical "free flying lessons" sign.

Right. On my "truth," as you put it.

Exactly. Perception *is* truth, but *only* in the absence of a personal experience. Suppose you sensed something, developed a feeling about it, and then immediately experienced it. Wouldn't that experience then influence your feelings in a deeper and more meaningful way and, thus, your subsequent thinking and decision making?

Of course, for example, if the owner of the sign invited me for a free flight in his plane.

Right, and told stories of his days flying corporate jets, and mentioned some very happy client experiences, and so on. And if the experience was positive enough, you'd probably even try to help him out by explaining your aversion to his "free flying lessons" sign and perhaps give him ideas on how to provide more and better value. You see, that's why I refer to this third step as "be real," and not "be believable." I don't want you to use *persuasion*-based believability as a proxy for *experience*-based believability. The more you can make your brand tangible and vivid to your audience, the stronger their feelings, memories, sense of affinity, and trust. So be as human and real as possible, in everything that you say and do.

That makes sense, but wasn't the sign a "real" part of the brand experience? There was certainly no artifice involved.

Vivid is real

It was "real," but it wasn't desirable; it did *not* exude value. Remember, customers make rapid, subconscious assumptions about value. Their brains make up their minds *before* they become aware of their decisions. They quickly assess a situation, and form a temporary hypothesis about what to do. And that's why *every* clue about your brand should be different *and* desirable *and* real *and* interesting, especially the more expressive, aesthetic ones that people use to quickly intuit value. You want the expectation of value to be apparent, as well as prime their subsequent experiences.

But what I want you to appreciate is that not all clues are created equal. Communication is good at framing the brand value and perhaps reinforcing it, but experiences will always have a greater impact on customers' beliefs and actions. Do you remember when we talked about searching for a car for your daughter to use to commute back and forth to college?

Sure. The frustrating, confusing, and mostly uninformed process, in which I eventually become overconfident in my decision. How could I forget?

You're a quick learner. So, let's suppose that after making that decision, but prior to actually purchasing the car, you're at a cookout chatting with friends, and you happen to mention your extremely well researched car choice. And at that point, one of your friends gawks at you and says, *"Did I hear you right? I would never buy that year and model car. My brother owned one and had nothing but problems. It was an absolute nightmare!"* Do you think that, after hearing that story, you'd move forward with your decision and buy the car anyway?

Probably not. What's your point?

You've made my point, which is simply this: people are more strongly influenced by anecdotal tales than they are by hours of research and mounds of data. Why? Because a personal story is more "real" to people, and thus more believable. And the more vivid the details of the story, the easier it is to "experience" it in your mind's eye and, therefore, the more credible it seems.

Data doesn't help create believability?

Of course it does, but only when helping to rationalize an existing belief or feeling. Or when the data is brought to life with vivid images and examples, such as in Al Gore's *An Inconvenient Truth*. You can *not* influence with data alone. In fact, various studies have shown that the *more* statistical information subjects were given about a brand or cause, the *less* engaged they became.

So point number one on the path to believability and trust is this: resist the urge to *persuade*, and instead look for ways to provide people with real, valuable, and vivid experiences with you and your brand. Allow customers to influence each other by using and displaying your brand, or by telling stories about their experiences, kind of like what's been going on with us for the past hour.

What? You mean our conversation?

[Tom smiling] Actually, I'm referring to how we've been subtly influencing each other's choices of food and beverages. Haven't you noticed?

Now that you mention it. I guess I've never really thought about marketing in that way.

You should start. It's much more effective than messaging, especially in today's skeptical marketplace, and given the influence of the Internet, with its global reach, ability to connect like-minded people, and powerful networking effect. Also, try to focus more on the aesthetic components of your customer touch points—the more vivid and emotional aspects—and less on the semantics. Let people intuit trust. They want to sell themselves on the value of your brand. They will resist attempts at being manipulated or sold, no matter how subtle or clever.

So whenever we sense that we're trying to communicate believability, we should figure out a way to demonstrate our value, or tell stories about it instead?

Or better yet, get your people, customers, and the media telling stories to each other. Strategically structure your organization around creating memorable experiences, which will provide customers with their own stories to tell. Instead of starting each day with boring, numbers-focused meetings, have your people share stories of how they *specifically* added value to customers' lives. And have your management team talk up these stories and reward the best ones. This simple practice will end up becoming self-perpetuating; your people and your customers will end up feeling good about each other, and it will elevate both brand expectations and execution.

Look, it's really this simple: The next time you're compelled to communicate, to send a message; the next time you feel the urge to plaster your name and tagline all over the place, make fantastic promises, or entice eyeballs . . . stop! Stop and ask: Is this adding value to our customers' lives? Get creative and figure out how to *demonstrate* your brand value by *adding* value. Do something to bring people together to experience that value, with you and with each other.

The end goal

Trust me: This is not as easy as it may sound. It requires a big shift in perspective, away from the idea that customers are the means to your goals, e.g. selling products, gaining eyeballs, making money, etc., to the new reality that customers *are* your end goal.

I'm not sure I see the distinction.

This is probably the toughest concept for business people to wrap their collective heads around. They've been conditioned to believe that the end goal of every business activity is . . . what?

To make money.

Right. And that's why they think transactionally and are obsessed with short-term performance and efficiency. They're conditioned to "charge" for everything, and they're always thinking about how to be smarter than people and use their connections and inside information to their financial advantage.

Like when the car salesperson says he has to take your offer to his manager "behind the curtain."

Right. Because he has all of the information. The new marketplace will *not* work that way. The car buyer of the very near future will walk into the "transactionally minded" dealership with a printout of exactly what she wants, when she wants it, and precisely what she is willing to pay for it.

What do you mean exactly by "transactionally minded?"

I mean organizations that are focused on manipulating the outcome, as opposed to ones that focus on the customer's process. The customer's process is what creates the desirable feeling. Think about what we're doing here. Isn't eating about the process? Sure it is. And so is lovemaking, reading, and theater. Relationships are ultimately about the process as well, the process of understanding, involvement, fairness, and reciprocity.

Look, being smarter than customers worked in the veiled marketplace of the past. Businesses used their inside information to gain an advantage over customers. The question was, how do we use money to get people to spend their money? It was all about advertising, salesmanship, and the art of persuasion. The goal was money, and the uninformed masses were the means to making money.

Today, the marketplace question is rapidly shifting to, how do we use money to bring people together to experience the value of our brand, to connect, exchange, learn, share, create, contribute, and ultimately, influence each other. The goal is to create happy customers, and the *means* is money.

Okay, but you're not suggesting that we stop advertising our products and services, are you?

Again, what I'm suggesting you do is to try to create connections with customers that don't *feel* like marketing or messaging. Create something *valuable*.

But don't people want *to know how we can help them?*

[Tom smiling and shaking his head] Here we go again. People don't want you to *tell* them how you can help them. Remember, they're already drowning in information and messages. Plus, it's one-way and controlled. So they feel talked to and directed, which is neither engaging nor believable. Instead, they want you to include them and engage them. They want you to prove that you are truly different, that you are doing what you do for their benefit.

Okay, I think I may be confused again.

Let me tell you why I think you, and many others today, are puzzled by this new way of thinking. Einstein once remarked, *"Perfection of means and confusion of ends seem to characterize our age."* It certainly characterizes today's world of marketing. Each and every day a plethora of new emails, articles, case studies and blogs promise to help marketers optimize everything from search engine rankings and viral video awareness to ad campaign engagement and direct mail response rates. Business books are popping up like weeds in a field (more than twenty new titles each day) expounding on how to be authentic, influence through social networks, create compelling blogs, spread sticky messages, and tell persuasive stories. There's only one problem: Trying to perfect this growing assortment of marketing vehicles (the "means") is causing brand confusion, and thus a negative effect on the goals of the enterprise (the "ends").

The end, the goal, of any organization, of any brand, is to create customers (or clients, users, members, donors, fans,) and you accomplish that goal by continually innovating to add value to their lives. Everything the organization invests in, and works on, should be laser focused to that end. Now, that may sound ridiculously evident, but I can assure you that it's not. For example, worldwide advertising expenditures will grow by a little over 6 percent this year to a whopping $473 billion! That's not to say that all advertising is valueless in the eyes of customers. But I can assure you that most of that $473 billion is worse than valueless; it's a drain on people's time, attention, and sensibilities.

And marketers keep spending all of that money on advertising because . . . ?

Why do marketers continue to fritter away their organizations' valuable time, attention and money trying to keep up with, and optimize, activities in which most customers find little, if any, value? And I'm not referring simply to advertising: I'd toss most direct mail, sales calls, brochures, "branding" projects, and PR into the heap as well. What keeps people grounded to their outdated mode of thinking about marketing and branding, thinking that creates nothing but inertia, waste, and confusion? I'll tell you what. Marketers are obsessed with words.

Excuse me?

Yeah, words. Marketers believe that they are in the communication and persuasion business. It's a lot easier than being in the value creation business. Plus, the process and results are subject to endless debate and are, therefore, much easier to hide behind. So, marketers self-servingly, and incorrectly, compare the marketing of products and services in a supersaturated marketplace to marketing a political candidate or making a legal case, where ambivalent people are forced to choose between two, and only two, alternatives. This self-motivated worldview has them fixated on doing things right—right message, right medium, right slogan, right tagline—blinding them to the most important marketing question: Are we doing the right things? The majority aren't.

I don't know. There's still a lot being written about the importance of brand names, elevator pitches, and positioning statements, among other things.

Don't take my word for it: Simply take a clear-eyed look at some of today's most successful and talked about brands. What are Nintendo and Harley-Davidson's slogans? Why doesn't Apple cover its packaging with persuasive copy? Can you tell me your financial advisor's "elevator pitch?" Did Toyota owners buy their vehicles because they wanted to "move forward?" Is that what caused the company to surpass GM in worldwide sales? Puh-lease. I own two Toyotas and I had to reach out to Google to discover that banal slogan. And speaking of Google, what the heck is their tagline anyway?

But surely words are important. We still need to communicate —on our website, during sales presentations, at events, etcetera.

I am not saying that words are unimportant. They can definitely add value when the *strategic intent* is to add value with words, and not merely to cajole, convince, or, heaven forbid, hypnotize people. But you are not in the words business; you're in the business of adding value to customers' lives. Resist the cognitive pull of communication and persuasion on your strategic thinking.

You are what you do (and why you do it)

Remember, desire, no matter how subtle, precedes information gathering. You want to draw people in with your look and feel, and have them quickly intuit value, competence, empathy, and passion. Like a trailer to a movie, you're trying to engage people in a condensed, intense experience that will motivate further examination that will support their initial feelings and thoughts.

So don't communicate your uniqueness, demonstrate it! If you try to entice or convince people with clever words or arguments, they'll instinctively judge and debate you, most likely in their heads, below *your* level of awareness. But if you draw them in with an experience or story, they'll become engaged; it will give those skeptical little voices in their heads something enjoyable to do.

That makes sense. But listen, regarding your movie trailer example, I typically read online reviews if I'm interested in "further examination" of a particular movie. I'm not really interested in what the studio has to say. So what does that mean for marketers?

Good point and an excellent question. What it means is that customers are always trying to sniff out the intention of communication. And you and I both know what they think of marketers' intentions, right? So impartial third-party endorsements will always be seen as more credible, which means that whatever "trailer" you do create had better be representative of your actual brand value. Remember, you don't control the "trip," and customers are actively searching for inconsistencies. So whatever they see, hear, and read about a "trip" with you had better be what they'll actually experience. Right?

We don't want to be like those glamour shots of fast food hamburgers, which, in reality, look like they've been used as seat cushions.

Not unless you're looking for someone to highlight the distinction on YouTube. Because I can assure you, they will.

So let me ask you a question about words, fully understanding that there are more vivid, and thus believable, ways to communicate our brand value?

You're finally beginning to appreciate cowboy wisdom. That's good.

Cowboy wisdom?

Yeah, cowboy wisdom says that the best sermons are lived, not preached.

That's a good one, and yes, I get it. Anyway, people are still going to listen to what we have to say, and read what we've written, so what should we be thinking about when we do communicate with words?

You should be thinking about the customer *mindset* that we've been discussing—overloaded, harried, and skeptical snackers, speed readers, and meaning makers—and design your content to attract and appeal to that mindset, as well as to your audience's sense of self and self-interest. Make it very easy for them to find and quickly experience what interests them. Do it in an engaging, yet efficient way. And keep in mind that you'll always be more interested in what you have to say than they will be.

So focus on their interests and desires—simplify everything.

Yes, but don't dumb it down or it will sound insulting. Remember, your audience's sense of self matters most. That said, use fewer words, but with greater impact. Say what everyone is thinking, but that no one has the guts to say. You want your customers to understand, but also to feel something. You want to frame your message for emotional impact, by using words that evoke the *right* feelings and create the desired expectation of value: different, desirable, real and interesting. Read what you've written, and if *you* don't feel anything, your customers probably won't either.

And as far as building trust?

Again, passion, intention, competency, and especially your look and feel are what convey trust. So first, and foremost, look the part; allow people to *perceive* the value of your offering. Then, communicate with excitement about them and their lives. Make relevant connections by providing *valuable* content and associations, and be open and honest and answer all of those *unasked* questions that are niggling at their minds.

Unasked questions? Like?

I don't know. What claims are you making or implying that may have your customers wondering about you, your offer, or your business model?

I don't really know.

Let me give you an example. Have you ever been to a Trader Joe's?

Sure.

Well, the next time you visit one, examine their signage. The company gives you reasons to believe in their low prices by posting words like, *"We manage all of our costs very carefully so we can pass our savings on to you."* Now, they are *not* trying to convey information. They're trying to answer the unasked question, and build trust and expectations. They're not trying to magnify the benefit; they're trying to make the benefit more "real." Does that make sense? Do you see the difference?

I think so. You're saying that we should tell people why we do what we do, as well as how we can do it?

Right, because if you don't, their skeptical minds will kick in: *"That's b.s."* or, *"That's what they all say."* It's like all of the "green" marketing taking place today. It's not "real" to most people, because it's not specific. Customers are pretty sure that they understand the brands' intentions. Do you see?

I see your point. We're trying to put people at ease, kind of like a physician speaking with a patient. Be human, honest, and empathetic. Ask questions and provide the right amount of information. Don't make light of the problem, but lighten up the situation.

That's exactly right—character, competence, and caring. Do I trust you? Do you know what you're doing? Do you care about me, as a person as well as a customer? Do you know how I'm feeling and what I'm thinking? Customers are drawn towards brands that empathize with them and are passionate about helping them improve their lives. And they're also drawn to brands that are confident, ones that have a strong point of view, but that don't take themselves so darn seriously.

Okay, but what if customers don't know what they need to know about the category and the brand? Then what?

In a word, education; like that caring physician, you may need to highlight some information for the customer. But—and this is a critical but—remember what the poet Yeats wrote, *"Education is not the filling of a pail, but the lighting of a fire."* So let *them* dig deeper and arrive at *their* answers. Don't speak down to them, and don't bury them with information to confuse and frighten them. It's like a dance. You attract them by being different and desirable—principally with your look and feel—and then you communicate a bit, easing their skeptical minds. Then you draw them in further with something interesting, desirable, and valuable. Then you provide a bit more information. Do you see what I mean?

I do. It's funny, but it sounds similar to how I surf the Internet.

That's a good example. In fact, try to structure your content like a web experience. The information should be immediate and transparent. Use short paragraphs with explanatory subheads. Keep the entire piece short and engaging, but offer directions to more content or conversations for people who choose to delve deeper into the subject. And please, please don't squeeze all of the life out of your words; get rid of all of the euphemisms, buzzwords, and corporate speak.

Remember, you're not trying to impress people. You're trying to connect with them, emotionally. So speak less and listen more. Communicate like a human being in a tone that expresses your brand aesthetics and value. Don't try to "manage" the conversation. Be confident, genuine, and caring and see where the conversation takes you. Relax, lighten up, and, for God's sake, slow down.

I sure wish I could slow down.

You can. And it's as easy as eliminating all of the activities that customers find value*less*. With all due respect, that's probably more than half of what you spend your time working on all day. Remember, customers develop an overall picture of your brand from everything that they experience. They don't usually perceive your brand in terms of its specific attributes. So dump the meaningless stuff, and focus intently on being different, effective, and meaningful.

And listen, when I say, *"be different, be desirable, be real, and be interesting,"* I'm not expecting you to evaluate your company or brand in that regard. Of course, like every other organization I've ever spoken with, you'll insist that you are. Instead ask, is this particular *activity* different, desirable, real, and interesting? Is this website different, desirable, real, and interesting? Is this sales call different, desirable, real, and interesting? Is this RFP different, desirable, real, and interesting? Everything! And if it isn't, then either do it differently or stop doing it (or outsource it), assuming, of course, that it doesn't matter to your customers. Anything less in today's marketplace will not get you and your organization to the happy now and happy life situation that *you're* looking for, if you follow my drift?

[Executive smiling] *I do.*

Interesting is interested

And now for the fourth, and most challenging, way of being: being interesting, keeping it fresh. Let me stress this one more time for good measure and, in keeping with our discussion, a little more vividly: the marketplace of old resembled a mass of caterpillars hanging around the tree of traditional media, venturing down the branches of mass distribution, and consuming the offshoots of brand advertisers. Being interesting back then was as straightforward as creating clever ads and being at eye level. No more. The masses have escaped their pupae, spread their distinctive wings, and are fluttering around fields blossoming with an abundance of colorful and succulent offerings. A fleeting glimpse is all you usually get of them.

So be interesting to attract them? Isn't that the same thing as "be different?"

We are way beyond attracting them. That was the first step: making your *brand* the target, the magnet that attracts the moving customers. You're being *interesting* to keep them emotionally invested in you, to keep them close to you and thinking about you. Being interesting is what you do to add value and meaning to the relationship *over time;* to reinforce their decision to believe in and choose you. You want them to assimilate the brand value, feelings, and meaning into their identities, so they won't be drawn away by something brighter and shinier in the future. Remember, this is not about attention and persuasion. That's old school branding. This is about attraction, value, trust, and affinity.

A few years back I wrote a little book that outlined ten truths for brand success. Truth number four was, *"From Interesting to Interested,"* where I wrote that, *"It doesn't matter what people think about you or your company. What matters is how you make people feel about themselves and their decisions in your presence."* And that's still true today. However, I now believe that by being *interesting*, you are appealing to your audience's *interests*; you're demonstrating that *your* interest lies with them. They're two sides of the same coin.

Being interesting is about trying new things. It's about setting an example. It's about tickling people's minds. The late, great mythologist, Joseph Campbell said, *"I don't believe people are looking for the meaning of life as much as they are looking for the experience of being alive."* Being interesting helps people feel alive through their association with you and your brand. When you're interesting, *they* feel interesting because of their association with you. Does that make sense?

It does. So why isn't "interesting" one of the components of your value chart?

Because being interesting should flow through the value components that you've chosen to strategically weave into your brand. Being interesting isn't simply about being clever and creative. It's about being wherever and whenever your audience is most receptive to your value components, and understanding and appealing to how they're feeling at that moment. It's about being interested in them and their lives and proving that you have their best interests at heart by doing interesting things that add value to their lives. It's about incessantly delivering value in exchange for their time and attention, since the key to long-term marketing success is to get them to come back for more, and to bring all of their friends.

So is being interesting the same thing as being innovative?

Yes, but not in some highbrow, academic way. Innovation can range from business model and supply chain innovation, to cost innovation, to logistics innovation, to designing new products and processes, creative pricing and financing, even to the way people answer the telephone and respond to emails. New ideas can be breakthrough or incremental. They can be significant game changers, or simple smile inducers. But they all have one thing in common: They're all about improving customers' experiences and lives. Have you ever heard of a hidden message or feature in a movie or computer program called an Easter egg?

I don't think so, no.

Remember Alfred Hitchcock's movies, and how he'd cunningly place himself somewhere in the film for a brief cameo appearance?

Yeah, and we'd try to find him.

Right. That's an example of an Easter egg. Often times,

computer programmers and game developers will add hidden jokes or features into their programs, then when a user executes some strange sequence of keystrokes or clicks, something unexpected happens. I remember once messing around with Google Maps, and I mapped driving directions from Boston to London. The directions said to *swim* 3,000 miles across the Atlantic Ocean.

I remember seeing something like that. Okay, I once noticed a line in the terms and conditions of my iPod Shuffle that read, "Do Not Eat iPod Shuffle." Is that like what you mean?

Yes, exactly. Now, most people would never refer to that as innovation, but I do. Any new idea that results in a more desirable customer experience, and which is believed will make the brand more valuable to everyone over time, I call innovation. Or, for the sake of keeping this really simple, call it "being interesting."

When Apple released new versions of its iPod and iPhone, it was interesting because it *improved* the customer experience. When they placed the *"Do Not Eat"* line on the packaging, it was interesting because it added value; it made people smile and gave them some social currency.

Look, it's compelling, and much simpler, to view a brand as some kind of fixed and valuable asset, like a piece of real estate, one that simply requires protection, promotion and occasional maintenance. But that won't work in today's marketplace. Instead, your brand needs to be constantly reinvented and refreshed to remain relevant. You should think of your brand as a perishable asset, like a salad bar.

Ask yourself, what changes have we made lately? What enticing value have we added today?

Don't let the brand become stale.

Never! You've got to continually shake things up; shatter your *own* patterns. Otherwise, you'll become like the hum of a fan to your audience. They'll eventually tune you out.

So surprise them with something interesting and valuable. That'll require a lot of work, not to mention a complete change of corporate mindset. But I can see how it will help, especially with our salespeople.

How's that?

It would give them a reason to contact people. They'll have something real and valuable to share, be it a new product, feature, a new service, or even just something interesting. Social value, as you referred to it.

Very true. But look, this takes a lot of organizational energy, imagination, and informality. It also takes a lot of guts, because being interesting isn't always about being nice, neat, and tidy. Sometimes you want to get customers questioning and wondering. You're trying to stimulate active cognitive involvement, a sense of puzzlement, and then discovery, which will enhance their interaction and bond with you and your brand. You're trying to provide your people and your customers with a shared sense of intimacy, mystery, surprise, and delight. You want to be upbeat, inviting, and different, and give them something to think about and talk about, as well as compel them to stay current with your doings and happenings.

How in the world are we supposed to manage all of those varied customer experiences?

The ultimate experience

You can't. But don't worry about it. By their nature, all marketplace experiences are unique to each customer and inherently unpredictable. You simply cannot foretell the future. You can't stage it for your customers, nor can they orchestrate it for themselves. There are too many variables. But you can understand how people construct stories through hindsight, how they organize their thoughts to create memories. And then, you may be able to help them create a story worth remembering, or even one worthy of sharing with their friends.

You see, we don't store a continuous, unedited, uncut version of the world around us. The mind doesn't record each and every detail of our experiences. Rather, it automatically trims life into smaller, more manageable, and meaningful scenes. It then edits and stores those scenes, and later retrieves them in a form something like a highlight film or movie trailer, one created by us and from our particular point of view. That final version of our story—that ultimate experience—is the one that matters to us most of all. Have you ever been engrossed in a movie, when suddenly, the screen goes black?

Yeah, during the last episode of The Sopranos.

[Tom smiling] No, I'm referring to a glitch of some kind.

Sure, I've had it happen.

Okay, now despite the popular notion that the disruption "knocked you out of your suspension of disbelief," you never really stopped believing that you were in a movie theater watching a movie. What it did was temporarily upset your movie-watching experience. The important question is, how did it affect your *ultimate* experience? The version that you created after the fact and stored in your mind.

It must not have affected it much, because I can't remember when it happened or the specific movie.

Exactly. There will always be elements of marketplace experiences that we'd rather have edited out—disrupted entertainment, inconvenience, trying to find what we're looking for, or not knowing what we're looking for. And relegating annoying scenes to the cutting room floor is a fully predictable enhancement to a customer's story. But, like preventing movie projector snafus, it is hardly the formula for creating a great story, one an audience will remember and rave about. That requires tapping into something much deeper and more meaningful, something that their minds can highlight in their personal movie trailers, something about themselves, and about their own role in their experiences. And that's where being interesting comes into play.

You see, today's commonly accepted view is that brands

tell us *their* stories with various products, pricing, people, online presence, facilities, and communications. That's a misguided view. In reality, we use our interaction with brands—their sceneries, props, set decorations, scripts, and actors—to construct our own stories, ones that we want to tell *about* ourselves. And since we define ourselves both according to what we identify with and what we reject, and given the abundance of marketplace choice, we now choose interactions which we feel will produce the best story possible. And we reject the others. Does that make sense?

So we're being interesting to enhance their *stories, not ours?*

That's exactly right. For example, as one particular story goes, each morning in the 1950s, noted advertising man David Ogilvy would stroll through New York City's Central Park on his way to his office. One beautiful April morning, he witnessed a man begging beside a sign that read, *"I am blind."* By evidence of the man's near empty cup, he was not doing very well. So, Ogilvy removed a marker from his briefcase and changed the sign to read, *"It is spring and I am blind."* After that small change, the money poured in.

Our simplistic, cause-and-effect way of viewing that story is that Ogilvy changed the message, thus making it more persuasive. In fact, what Ogilvy did was much more subtle and powerful. Ogilvy changed the prop: he made it different, desirable, real, and interesting. And, by doing so, he influenced the scene and the story creation of every passerby. By *strategically* adding those three simple words—*"It is spring*"—he brought life to the scene, encouraged empathy in the actors, and helped them create a story about themselves: a story that made them feel good about themselves and their actions.

Wow, I never would have thought of it like that.

That, my friend, is what building a strong brand is all about today. Sure it's about being different and creating desire and preference. But it's also about evoking compassion, passion and pride. It's a philosophy that both bonds people to your brand and one that gets you, and your people, up in the morning! Goethe said it, *"The hardest thing to see is what is in front of your eyes."*

Like this notion that it doesn't matter what customers think about us, but rather how we make them feel about themselves and their identity stories.

Yeah, and like that check sitting right there in front of you. Are you ready to get out of here?

Absolutely!

Great. One last thing while you wait for your receipt: Do you like puzzles?

Who doesn't?

Okay, here's one of my favorites: A marketer dies and is traveling down the road to brand heaven, when she reaches a fork in the road. One of the roads continues on to brand heaven, but the other goes straight to commodity hell.

Standing at the fork are two identical twin brothers who also happen to be advertising guys. One of the brothers always tells the truth and the other always lies, but the marketer has no idea who is who. She is allowed to ask only *one* question to only *one* of the brothers to find the road to brand heaven. What one question does she ask that reveals the answer, and what road does she take and why?

Which road is the road to brand heaven?

Remember, she doesn't know if she is talking to the liar or to the truth teller.

Hmm . . . that's right. Okay . . . wait, that won't work. Okay, so what's the one question?

Go to *www.acleareye.com* and click on my smile in the photo to get the answer.

Walk the talk.

And have fun doing it! Good luck and stay passionate!

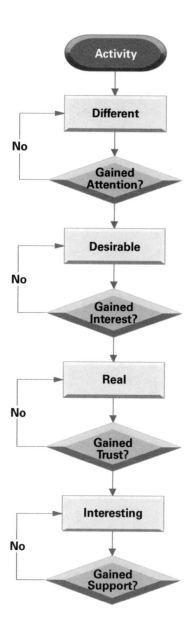

The difficulty of literature is not to write,
but to write what you mean.

Robert Louis Stevenson

Afterword

When I first outlined this little book, I worried about whether I had thought enough about why and how customers make decisions. Did I take everything into consideration? The more I thought about it, the more I realized that I couldn't really take everything into consideration, because all of the variables in any marketplace decision are incalculable. That said, I do hope that I've written what I meant to write; that I've clearly articulated today's changing economic and cultural environment, and provided some insights that help you examine and enhance the value of your brand.

I've been sharing this evolving model of brand as expectation, as a proxy for value and self-esteem, with various audiences over the past few years, listening for objections, confusion and, most importantly, insights. I've addressed business-to-business companies, financial service firms, well-known telecommunications brands, global nonprofits, consumer products giants, advertising and media companies, and beverage behemoths. And they all seem to get it, which is great. But I want to be clear about something.

My *business* philosophy is based on my belief that our western society has turned its attention away from the future toward the near term, so most people use the marketplace as a diversion. They approach it with an emotional logic. They want to experience novelty, and the pleasures of consumption, leisure and well-being. They want to lose themselves in new challenges and experiences, control their personal near-term futures, and better themselves physically and mentally. They want to feel good about themselves and their decisions, and so they're constantly on the lookout for something that suits them better in those pursuits.

Our modern marketplace is driven by this egoistic, searching behavior that wants more and faster seduction, instant satisfaction, entertainment, change, fashion, stimulation, innovation, ad infinitum. And the way to succeed in business today is to tune in to this new consumer reality and to be better at orchestrating and delivering that "value."

But here's the rub: although I understand this to be the nature of our individualistic, do-it-yourself, better oneself, and be happy economy, I'm not saying that the marketplace is the path to happiness in the long-term. In fact, studies suggest that we are generally less happy today than when we had less. It's a paradox. So yes, I do teach how to appeal to today's consumer psyche in order to be successful in the marketplace for products, services, entertainment, and ideas. But no, I'm not saying that your products or services are *necessarily* going to make people happier in the *long-term*. I'm not that naïve (although I do believe that a strategic focus on providing happiness will help immensely). I'm more inclined to believe in a much simpler path to happiness: having something to do, someone to love, and something to look forward to.

In any event, thank you for allowing me to share my views with you through my writing. My only wish is that it has inspired you to be more curious, caring, honest, and fearless, and that you will help spread this message through your caring influence and associations. And if there is ever any way that I can help you in your endeavors, please don't hesitate to let me know. I leave you with a quote by English photographer Cecil Beaton, which perfectly sums up my philosophy, "Be daring, be different, be impractical, be anything that will assert integrity of purpose and imaginative vision against the play-it-safers, the creatures of the commonplace, the slaves of the ordinary." Stay passionate!

About the Author

Tom Asacker is often described as a catalyst, and a nonconformist. He is an independent brand strategy advisor and an internationally acclaimed speaker. He is also the author of *A Clear Eye for Branding: Straight Talk on Today's Most Powerful Business Concept* and *Sandbox Wisdom: Growing Your Business with the Genius of Childhood*.

Beyond his success as an author and speaker, Tom is a former corporate executive and an accomplished entrepreneur. He is a recipient of the George Land Innovator of the Year Award; holds medical patents and product design awards; and is recognized by *Inc.* magazine, MIT, and the Young Entrepreneurs' Organization as a past member of their Birthing of Giants entrepreneurial executive leadership program.

Today, Tom helps professionals and organizations grow their brands by connecting deeply with the feelings of their audiences and creating value that truly improves their lives. You can find out more about Tom and his philosophies by visiting *www.acleareye.com*.